The City of Light Sedona
Revelation of the Prophecies, Purpose, Plans and Manifestation of Cities of Light, Love and Healing

By Genii Townsend
with Charles Betterton

Edited by Kathie Brodie and Renee Trenda

Copyright 2011 Sedona Light Center, Inc.

Published by CENTER SPACE™
(Center for Spiritual, Personal And Community Enlightenment)

Limits of Liability and Disclaimer of Warranty

The author and publisher of this book and the associated materials have used their best efforts in preparing this material. The author and publisher make no representations or warranties with respect to the accuracy, applicability, fitness, or completeness of the contents of this material. They disclaim any warranties expressed or implied, merchantability, or fitness for any particular purpose.

The author and publisher shall in no event be held liable for any loss or other damages, including but not limited to special, incidental, consequential, or other damages. If you have any doubts about anything, the advice of a competent professional should be sought. This material contains elements protected under International and Federal Copyright laws and treaties. Any unauthorized reprint or use of this material is prohibited.

And the City had no need of the sun, neither of the moon to shine in it . . . For the glory of God did lighten it.

Revelation 12:23

Table of Contents

What In Heaven Is Going On? 8

Once Upon a Once There Was a Beginning 10

Out of The Closet After 25 Years, Imagine That! 16

The City of Light Proclamation! 17

A Moment of Quantum Awakening 18

First to Go Galactic. . . The City of Light Sedona 20

Welcome to the New Jerusalem! 22

Beginning City of Light Plot Plan Information 24

The City of Light Plot Plan 25

Hermes, Architect of the City of Light Sedona 26

Importance of the City of Light High Towers and Gate Towers 28

The City of Light Gate Towers 30

The City of Light High Towers 31

Genii's Interior City of Light Visits 32

Visiting the City 34

Genii Experiences the City of Light – Vision Visit 1 36

Part # 2 Second Visit – The Energy Park 37

Part # 3 Third Visit – Meeting with My City Guide 38

City Interior Visit- The Reflection of a New Beginning 39

City of Light Tour – The Fountain of Light 41

Filling In the Blanks 43

The Empowerment Emporium 45

Visit to the City of Light Birth-aterium 47

The Deciding Place 49

The Institute of Image Imprinting 51

The Star Wings of a Healing Building 52

The Playing Field 54

Healing the Future through the City of Light 55

UFO Visitors 57

UFOs and The City of Light 58

Of UFOs and Human Fears 59

Cities of Light – The Genii Connection Report 60

Seeing Cities of Light through Many Eyes 62

Time Warp 63

Planet Peace Time Line 65

A New World Now In Progress 67

A Universal Cosmic Community 69

More About a Universal Cosmic Community 71

The Feminine Place 73

The Feminine Rejuvenation Temple 76

Inner Workings Beneath The City Of Light! 78

Space Scientific Advancement 79

The Be-ing Building 81

The City of Light Appears, Now What? 83

Introduction to the City's Embassy of Peace Headquarters 86

Genii's Visits to the Embassy of Peace Headquarters 87

Of War and Peace 89

Additional Connection from La-Luke 91

The Council of Master Minds Meeting 1 92

Conversation with A Commander of Space Light 94

The Cosmic Raising of Consciousness 97

Somewhere in Non-Time 100

Of the President, Genii's Talents and Advancement 103

Cosmic Dream Makers! 106

Betwixt And Between Earth Growth! 108

Energy Healing With Genii and Roger 110

A Time for Light 113

From Time to Time 115

The Light of Interest 118

The Big One! 121

Contact! 124

Out With the Old And In With the New 126

Of Upheaval and Staying Balanced 128

Today is the Tomorrow of Yesterday 130

On The Road Again 133

The Planeteers 135

Upward and Onward 137

Going the Distance 140

Community of Cosmic Dwellers 143

Seeing the Unseen 146

Speaking the Language of Space 148

Somewhere Between Heaven and Earth Where Magic Never Ends 150

Do You Speak Space? 152

The Magic Advantages of Light 155

World Changes Ready or Not!	158
Cosmic Communities and Such	162
And It Came Upon A Midnight Clear!	165
A Closing Embassy of Peace Message	167
In the Wonder of It All . . .God Is!	168
Other References to Sedona as a Sacred Site	171
The History of New Age Sedona as a Sacred Place	172
The Sedona Report on Spaceports	173
Sedona and The Celestine Prophecy by James Redfield	174
Sacred Sites, Sedona by Shirley MacLaine	175
Appreciation for Shirley MacLaine	177
Loving the Planet and Each Other	178
A Second Age of Universal Creation	182
The Near Death Experience and the City of Light	185
Fourteen Etheric Cities of the Earth	196
An Intentional Community as A City of Light	199
About the Author	202
Introduction to the Light Center	203
Invitation from Genii and The Light Center	205
Training Programs with Genii	206
The 4 Keys to Light	207
Introduction to Ultimate Destinyland™ and Ultimate Destiny University	209
Featured Resources from Ultimate Destinyland™	210
Introduction to CENTER SPACE™ Resources	211

What In Heaven Is Going On?

Once upon a once, God said ...

Once upon a once, the Great Creator looked over the creation of stars, galaxies, and planets, and said: "Yes, this is God good!"

Suddenly, an angel appeared and said, "Perhaps you might want to take a look at that blue planet over there." And the angel pointed to this planet.

God took a closer look and saw a planet in upheaval. Wars and threats of wars, people against people, and pain everywhere—and they were sending fireworks back into the universes!

"Oh my, this will never do," God said. "Hmmm, what is to be done to bring peace once and for all?"

Then God got an idea, a very big, magnificent idea. "Yes, that will work! First, I must get their attention, and then I'll work on the peace end. For this planet must be healed. I will send my angels and lightworkers to set the scene.

It will be my most magnificent production ever witnessed on that planet. I shall design and bring forth a glorious healing edifice and all will see for the first time in their history my CITY OF LIGHT that will have within it my holiness, and ways of healing unknown there."

"Yes, I agree with me! I shall send forth my light to do the healing with my love. Angels, take down this Proclamation and send it forth to be picked up by those who are open to receive such good God news. Let's see, how shall I begin? Oh, yes …"

"**My PROCLAMATION**! Yes, that is a good start …"

"**Take heed, oh people of the Earth. There will come by dawn's early light a new heaven on earth that embodies all I stand for. Love shall be my messenger and my Light shall perform the healings.**"

"**This demonstration is now declared in process and is given as a gift to every living soul who inhabits your planet (which, incidentally, belongs to me.) Make not an unbelief of this declaration, for I make the earth with my insignia of love. No longer will wars and unsettlement be tolerated! Only peace shall be your reward. This decree cannot be stopped under any circumstances, as I stand as the Creator and vow this to be so!**"

"And now … Take heed, each one who is reading or hearing this. Know that Peace on Earth is my intent and all will know my words are true and demonstrated. For you will see for yourself in your third dimension. Prepare yourself for such a demonstration, as it is nearing the sunrise of expectancy. Awaken, for it is time!"

Signed,

God!

Once Upon a Once There Was a Beginning

The following is a written testimonial of what took place in my learning of the "City of Light". It is written in my words, including my feelings, as we went into and thru this discovery.

I stand by every word as my truth that is so engrained within me that I am the embodiment of the Holy City of Light. Enjoy or toss, it makes no difference, for what you are about to learn about will come to pass, ready or not.

In love and blessings,

Genii Townsend

Little did I know when I married Rev. Dr. William (Bill) J. Townsend in 1978 in the Apple Valley, California, Church of Religious Science (RS) what an adventure we had in store for us. Not in my wildest imagination could I come up with such ideas. I was just a first year RS student from North Hollywood, California who delighted in the teaching of how I could better my life, which I had requested of God after a divorce.

Rev. Dr. William Townsend

About a year later we were guided to leave there and go to Las Vegas, which was not my favorite place to live by any means, but it was thought that my career of puppet and marionette performing could be an advantage, due to stage productions Vegas style, and I made a lot of celebrity marionettes to fill the bill.

Well, that was not why we were guided to be in Vegas, but rather to open a "Light Center" type church, which we did. That was not surprising due to Dr. Bill being a leading minister for some time in the movement.

One day after service a lady told us that a friend of hers in another state was coming to Las Vegas and was guided to talk to Dr. Bill. She said he was a channel. I had some idea from some silly movies that tables would dance and ghosts would come forth and I was not in any way, shape or form into that! I was a student of truth, after all!

Dr. Bill decided it would be all right, and because he was a meditation teacher and knew a lot more than this first year student, I said okay but I would have a room full of people, a tape recorder going, and it must be in the day time to light up that room.

Everything I wanted was set up so this person who did weird things would be able to deliver his message, whatever it was, when he arrived. He did arrive with his wife which made me feel better because I was thinking he was attached to someone who must be grounded, I hoped.

A gentle artist entered, who proceeded to not only change his voice as he talked, but his features as well. To me this was astonishing, and so much so I was not hearing what was being said until nudged from within; "Pay attention!" So I did, and I learned many truths that resonated with me enough that I began to relax and absorb.

Nothing of a grand nature was said until the next day when we went for a ride north, and it was here that we first heard about a City of Light, as he described it, when he had us stop at a specific location. Of course I could not see anything and neither could Dr. Bill, but what the heck, dreamers can envision anything. So that was the message. We said thanks and this man left, taking his multi-dimensional personage with him, and that was pretty much that.

What interested me so much was the way the first meeting with him took place; a wife asking questions of her husband who was someone else (not a normal meeting in my thinking). I began to wonder about the way it was done. Dr. Bill was a deep meditation teacher so I asked him if he could do something like that where I could ask the questions and record the answers. Sounded like fun and I like fun so . . .

With him agreeing, we quickly set a time and proceeded to begin. Talk about sticking your neck out! I had no idea what would take place, much less what questions to ask.

I was hanging in mid-air when a few minutes later a strange voice came through Dr. Bill. Question? What question? Who has questions? Me?

When I found my voice I said, "Hi. Well, sort of."

This, then, was the beginning of many years of questions and answers from a floor and tape recorder position for me, and the "I'm not here" couch position of Bill.

A few months into this way of learning thru questions and answers and then replaying the tape back to Bill so he could hear what came through, he was guided to obtain some art supplies, a drawing board and do some sketching.

Since Bill only had mechanical drawing in school he was a perfect candidate, so for three years he brought through the plans of this City of Light, so-called, that the first visionary said he saw, for Bill had no personal thoughts of how it should be.

Not that Bill really wanted to do this. He would "come out" periodically and say "I'm not doing this anymore", at which time he was promptly sent back into the guest room to continue bringing forth this artwork.

When all was said and done, the results turned out to be architectural drawings and directions for this "City of Light". At first we thought we were to build it ourselves until wisdom entered to inform us that not only did we not have the building material here, but no building code would permit it to be built under any circumstances. That pretty well set that in cement, so this had to be something in another dimension that somehow was to come forth here like magic.

The City of Light, we were informed, was to be a "City of Light Healing", a place where people would come to be healed of whatever needed healing, thru the medium of light frequency attention, meaning no knives to be cutting into the human body light lines, and no needles to scare the kids and adults as well. Count me in too!

This would be done in what is called "the light modules" of advanced technology where peace would reign supreme and no stress would even think of entering. In that setting, the patient would receive the necessary light frequencies and vibrations to heal their particular ailments.

Several year later, Genii was given directions on creating a lesson plan called The 4 Keys to Light, wherein she teaches students how to become Light Technicians. These practitioners could assist people in their healing by connecting them to the Healing Light facilities of the City of Light. These treatments would take place outside of the City of Light, and there would be no charge to those being served.

In watching the plot plan of this city come forth, it looked a little like a storybook fantasy, some parts of which are familiar to us, but with advanced scientific technology that would send Star Trek writers back to the drawing boards.
For example, there is a 1,500 foot High Tower that is designed to catch UPPC's (Uniphase Power Capsules) that have been bombarding this planet for eons of time, thus lighting the City of Light and a zillion other areas it can reach.

To me this indeed would have to be a God-made miracle as I saw no other way it could happen, and surely it is needed on this planet at this time in history.

It has been 10 years since Dr. B made his transition, leaving me to carry the ball, so to speak, and all this time the plans and information have been secretly protected in their holiness. Before he left I was trained to trans-audio (channel) information, thus keeping me up on the current progress. When Dr. Bill departed, I was literally pushed to move to Sedona with my daughter, Starr-Light Taylor. I didn't know why then.

Now after living here for a few years and having the experiences shared in this publication, I know it was and is my ultimate destiny to be here in Sedona to introduce The City of Light.

Throughout this publication and in the related Resources for Empowerment and Enlightenment catalogue, I have included other books, audio video programs and other resources you might find interesting. Because I have found so much value from The Starseed Transmissions and The Third Millennium by Ken Carey, I have included his works in the Resource Directory and an article from the mid 1990's Ken gave to Randy Peyser.

I wish to thank the many other mentors who have helped me grow in ways I never knew were possible:

Many thanks to Shirley MacLaine who stood by her beliefs no matter what. As I move forward announcing the City of Light, I too may be "out on a limb" but to stand with my beliefs no matter what. Her book stretched me to learn that I could be and see more than I ever thought I could. Thanks Shirley.

To Ernest Holmes and the Church of Religious Science where I learned that he said to listen to the wee voice inside. So I went looking and listening and what came of it was and is all the trans-audio writings in this book. Thanks Dr. Holmes for giving me the insights to go inside and find a few friends in high places that have brought me to this day in a very unusual way. I found the voices!

To Dr. Bill Townsend with whom I got all the fringe benefits of his love and his teachings. Thanks 'B' it was a great ride which looks like it is still rolling.

To Charles Rhinehart who invested time and effort to introduce me to what a channel was, and just how good a channel can be. He was that and more! Thanks Charles and Lavetta too for permission to use Charles' painting of the City of Light.

To Master Yoda who makes me know that the Power of the Force is just to "Believe" and to use the Jedi energy to assist others and as a Jedi Master I do what I can and give thanks for the constant reminder with my Lightsaber.

To Kermit the Frog who helped me find my own Rainbow Connection thru fun and laughter, wisdom and love. Thanks Kermy… you really are a Prince of a Frog!

To Walt Disney whose mind I can walk thru at Disneyland and embody all the fun and imagination he thought up and the belief that Wishes and Dreams do come true. Thanks Mr. D. I'll see you next time on the green bench on Main Street. You were and are the greatest. Thank you!

To Joel Osteen who daily lifts me thru his uplifting wisdom via video, tapes and books and fun comments. I am pleased to follow his wisdom and uplifting advice. Thanks Rev. Joel

To Lynn Grabhorn who grabs me by the collar daily and says it like it is, leaving no doubt in my mind that the Law of Attraction is correct. Thanks Lynn wherever you are, you are an angel.

To Kathie Brodie close friend, and mentor who clears the thought processes when they become jammed with the past and corrects my writing errors for a final read out. Thanks Kathie you are loved...deep.

To my business partner Charles Betterton who requests no acknowledgements or accolades. While sharing time and efforts with him, he has made this manuscript what it is intended to be and opened my mind to the values of the Inter-net for my inner-net connections. He has done this in love, applying his expertise to move it forward in appreciation of what God has given him to do and this is a big one...me and my guidance.

I am truly the recipient of his wisdom and peach iced tea and the pleasure of teaching him that 'fun' really is a part of growing, and Disneyland fills that lesson well. Thanks partner. It is a pleasure to serve with you in light and love in this higher connection with Spirit.

To my loving family Alan, Starr-Light, Dave, Ginger, Dougie, and even my dog Clancy who was a teacher of great furry wisdom and my new puppy Light Spirit for all the lessons you have taught me known or unknown in growing and permitting me to do what God has intended me to do in the overall picture. Love you all and hopefully left out none.

To Mary Ann and Mike Bishop of Sedona Copy and Design Center whose friendship has brought me many heart treasures as well as the second printing of this book. You are truly the best of the best!

And last but not least, to all the celebrities that I have had the pleasure of recreating in miniature form that hang around my home to be performed or given away as gifts in thanks for something they have given me: Carol Burnett, Sammy Davis Jr., Deepak Chopra, Mark Victor Hansen, Les Brown, Liza Minnelli, Barry Manilow, Nathan Lane, Whoopi, Ellen, Oprah, President Jimmy Carter, President and Mrs. Obama and the list goes on.

So I feel better now saying thanks with more to come.

There are a lot more and I thank each and everyone even all the thousands of kids and parents that came to celebrate at Geniiland.

Love and Blessings to each and every one.

Genii

PS. This publication is a work in progress. Some of the wording received in the audio transmissions may seem strange but I have left them as I received them.

While initial editing and proof reading have been performed, (mostly thanks to Kathie Brodie and Renee Trenda), please do share any typos you find or suggested clarifications with me. The blog site where you may provide your feedback and suggestions is at http://sedonacityoflight.wordpress.com/.

Out of The Closet After 25 Years, Imagine That!

The City of Light Sedona: Revelation of the Prophecies, Purpose, Plans and Manifestation of Cities of Light, Love and Healing

In this publication, Genii shares information she has kept secret for 25 years. The book describes several prophecies, the purpose and plans for a City of Light. Included are diagrams and descriptions of advanced "Light Healing Technologies", discussion of the need for spiritual awakening and enlightenment on earth, and Sedona's past and future "ultimate destiny" as a City of Light. They include many detailed drawings drafted over a period of about seven years by the late Rev. William Townsend. The drawings are based on guidance and direction he received from Inner Guidance while in a trance state similar to Edgar Cayce's readings now maintained by the Association for Research and Enlightenment.

These documents and recordings are being transferred to a digital format. The contents can then be more readily accessible for ongoing research and development of possible training programs based on the information they contain.

Genii with the "Treasure Chest" of hundreds of cassette tapes, thousands of pages of transcriptions and scores of detailed drawings and designs of every facet of the City of Light.

The City of Light Proclamation!

THERE IS COMING FORTH ON THIS CONTINENT A NEW NATION,
BATHED IN LIGHT IT STANDS ON A NEW FOUNDATION OF
TRUTH AND HONOR, A CITY OF LIGHT!

IT HAS BEEN BUILT BY BEINGS OF LIGHT INTELLIGENCE.
IT IS PURE AND UNDEFILED. WHEN IT IS REVEALED TO THE MASSES,
IT WILL HERALD IN A NEW ERA
NEVER BEFORE EXPERIENCED ON THIS PLANET.

THOSE WHO VENTURE THERE, WILL RETURN HOME
ADVANCED IN THOUGHT AND EMOTIONS SO TRUE
THAT THEY WILL CHANGE THOSE AROUND THEM
WITHOUT LIFTING A FINGER.

THE CITY OF LIGHT WILL ATTRACT AND REPEL.
THOSE WHO WILL BE ATTRACTED ARE THOSE WHO SEEK A HEALING.
THOSE WHO ARE REPELLED, ARE THOSE WHO HAVE
CHOSEN TO PLAY IN THE DARKNESS FOR YET A WHILE.

IT IS IN THIS LIGHT APPEARANCE THAT THE WORLD
AS YOU KNOW IT WILL BE NO MORE.....EVER!
THEN SHALL COME THE PEACEMAKERS WHO WILL SPREAD THIS LIGHT
THROUGHOUT THE LANDS AND CHANGE THE FREQUENCIES AROUND
THOSETHEY COME IN CONTACT WITH AS IF TOUCHED BY ANGELS.

THERE ARE HUMAN "LIGHT BEINGS" NOW BEING GROOMED
THAT WILL TAKE THEIR PLACE IN THE CITY PROPER
LONG BEFORE THE CITY IT SELF APPEARS.

WHEN THE REVELATION OF THE CITY OF LIGHT APPEARS
IT WILL SEEM LIKE THE SECOND COMING TO MANY.
IN REALITY, IT IS THE FIRST COMING
AND NOTHING ELSE IS NEEDED.

IT IS IMPERATIVE THAT THOSE WHO WANT
TO BE PART OF THIS PRECEDING HAPPENING
NOW ADDRESS THEIR WISHES TO THEIR GUIDING INTELLIGENCES
THAT HAVE THEM IN THEIR CHARGE.
YOUR WORLD IS IN A PROCESS OF DRAMATIC CHANGE.
ALL IS NECESSARY TO BRING IN THE CITY OF LIGHT!

Received by Genii Townsend. © 2008 by The Light Center. All rights reserved.

A Moment of Quantum Awakening

From *The Third Millennium* by Ken Carey

"At the moment of quantum awakening, change will occur rapidly, rippling across the terrestrial surface like a wave. Everything in earth's gravitational field will be affected in some way. There will be time of massive change, a change on a scale that has no Historical precedent.

Properly understood, these changes and their coming have the ability to inspire a degree of hope and optimism unprecedented in the history of your race, for they spell the end of humankind's subconscious condition and therefore portend, as the scriptures foretell, an end to bloodshed, starvation, warfare, exploitation, and needless suffering.

The consciousness that is awakening upon this world is no respecter of Darwinian values. Its perception brings new values and new ways of being. During these decades you are seeing the decent of the Angels of Healing. Even now they are incarnating.

Every individual who becomes a clear and undistorted channel for eternal love into these times offsets a thousand who remain locked in the dissolving values of the old. You are already living in the dawning hours of the age of planetary awakening, the age of peace and community building.

The future as always holds an element of surprise but there have been those in both east and west who have known a 'due date' during the second decade of the 21st century. Do not discount the possibility that the moment might come as a thief in the night. And, do not be one of the foolish who will wait until the last moment to come to terms with the rising awareness.

This will be an important occasion! The event will be of a greater power than any earth has ever seen. More energy will be released in a few moments than is typically released upon the earth surface in many years. This energy will take the form of heightened perception and deepened emotional connection, rejoining the individual and God……"

Journeying Into the City of Light, Imagine That!

Once in the middle of Genii's ordinary life, God gave her a mission like no other she had ever heard of. Now you are invited to journey with her into....

The City of Light Sedona

Just Imagine

... entering a place of such beauty that it makes you an instant believer that anything is possible, like entering a 5 story-high gate that is encoded with your personal beliefs that make you feel like you just came home.

... experiencing healing techniques in Light modules where no drugs, knives, or needles can sever the body's electrical lines.

... entering a 'Memory Manor' building where you can release past memory hurts with no emotion attached.

... standing by a Fountain of Light that makes you feel great, and sitting on benches that massage your body.

... taking a dip in a healing pool that can clear skin conditions.

... being able to balance your emotions in an Empowerment Emporium.

.... seeing babies being born in a Birth-aterium, laughing with the mother who had no anesthesia, no pain and the only crying would be for the pure joy of the experience.

...entering a stadium-size building called The Embassy Of Peace Headquarters where Light Beings from the Universe gather to help bring forth Peace on this Earth.

IS ANY OF THIS POSSIBLE?

IT'S NOT ONLY POSSIBLE... BUT PROBABLE!

First to Go Galactic... The City of Light Sedona

What is the Sedona Galactic Healing City of Light Connection?

"The prophecy is that indeed this power center of earth has been chosen as the first kick-off location that has its opening imprints of a City of Light Healing. This is important due also to the technology coming forth as the impact of this energy rises and those now in process feel the peak of final preparation whose light work on themselves is reaching its own peak."

Photo of "Spaceship in Clouds" over Coffee Pot Rock in Sedona © OceAnna Laughing Cloud

"The inner cleansing opens the way for the planet's changeover, and it will be seen as totally completed. Ready or not, the light frequencies of the Sedona areas pull in yet more power. As those who live there attempt to stay balanced, the wake of this ballistic cosmic energy leads the holy demonstration. Many of your current scientists would be astonished at the impact this silent yet powerful motion will have on the total planet."

What does it mean to go Galactic?

"To go Galactic means to be first to be enlightened to such a degree that the energy forces maneuver the opening to the heavens so quickly that the electromagnetic fields of upper and lower connection spread its frequencies throughout the rest of the planet in a second of your so-called time. It is within this starting point of Cosmic Light that it targets this planet through, in particular, the Sedona portal. In this way the Cosmic Connection is made."

"Since what has just been said is important, are you ready for this Connection of L I G H T?"

**All is in process. It is here … it is now …
We bid you the Light of the eternal day, in Peace and in Love …
So Light it Be!"**

OceAnna Laughing Cloud is a Spiritual Alchemist, Visionary Artist and Cosmic Dolphin, who lovingly creates from the Heart of Creation to bring forth her gifts to humanity to promote Eternal Peace, Love and Harmony. Her Living Waters of Creation™ and Vibrational Photography assist in bringing forth the Hidden Realms of Creation by way of portals of illuminating, which assist in awakening to that which has always been present, namely Oneness and Unity Consciousness. OceAnna's mission is to teach through the language of Eternal Light and Frequency, the importance of the Holy Sacrament of Water and its paramount importance to Mother Earth. Her latest offerings can be accessed on her website www.heartofthedeepbluesea.org.

Sedona Is the Chosen Place

"Sedona, Arizona has been chosen! It is bringing the dawn of a new awakening. Sedona is empowered to be the first to bring in the new Spiritual Power Center never before experienced on this planet!"

"It will serve all who seek enlightenment on a level never before experienced on this planet. It will fill the void that many have sought for eons of time…the time is now!"

"Awaken…for it is time for all Light Workers to band together as one with their varied talents, growth systems and the making of a new design ready to be put into action, not just for some but, for all."

"The City of Light Sedona is a center court of high esteem and acknowledgement ready to move forward in bringing forth an edifice of such magnitude, that to see it, one would be awe struck and changed beyond changing. It is that magnificent!"

"The Genii has known for some time that this Divine obsession of the Divinity was in place for the unveiling when the pyramid designer decrees this to take place. As the changes take place on your planet enough to permit the unveiling of the City of Light, Dimensions will part and move away like a stage opening production and the people will fall to their knees in Holy Communion. The unbelievers will for the most part, depart, returning when their elevation of frequencies can adhere to the vibrations they have just witnessed."

"Why Sedona you might ask? The power stations here known as Vortexes hold much more than a slight frequency that humans can sense to a minute degree (which is filtered, due to the nerve freeways you carry.) The Vortexes carry Light from other levels and dimensions that can only be perceived by a few now, never the less, this is accurate to a minute detail. The Light coming through the vortexes makes it possible for the City of Light to demonstrate."

"So then, it would seem that this Sedona area is a place of honor and Sacred beyond belief, as will be seen by the world of your planet as the time so called, races to meet its destiny…. The City of Healing Light!

So Light it Be!"   January 1, 2005

Welcome to the New Jerusalem!

As the planetary changes flood our senses and we work to stay in balance trying to keep normal, yet within our knowing that something is going on, I have asked this question of my inner teachers.

Why a City of Light?

Answer: "In the light of all that takes place in your world, as upheaval makes more of the same, it would look as though peace cannot come into being, which of course is nonsense."

"The predictions of generations entwined in past events, have tucked into the collective memory of all people, certain expectations that have the power to produce enough pre-programming of what is being experienced with confused mentality and negatively induced as truth. This is coming to an end. Enough! "

"For centuries, this same time warp has produced war after war after war instead of a constant peace which was given as a gift from the Creator in the beginning. This gift has been misused as constant ego-generated thoughts produced conflict and turmoil. Thus love must be wedged in to be of assistance."

"As generation after generation said they wanted peace, war was declared instead as a force to be dealt with. And war in the name of whatever any particular person deems the Creator of all was deemed a way to peace."

"Chaos on this planet is experienced on a consistent basis. Since this was not the original intent and with mankind not able to bring forth its own peaceful loving ways, it is now moved into a higher level of progress, which is somewhat out of your hands."

"What, losing control? What has been achieved so far on your own? Is not the cry to the Creator for peace on Earth good will to men? A Primal Source is needed to expel the darkness (ignorance) and bring Light into this planet, which must live and function with others more evolved in a balanced universe. Thus the City of Light is now being brought to the forefront, which demonstrates and bears fruit of loving kindness and healing facilities advanced in techniques that are unknown on this planet."

"Those who, for whatever reason, cannot move forward in the ultimate destiny of this planet, will be in for quite a surprise as they witness the intervention of Light."

"So there has been talk of a massive change in 2012, and rightly so. However, this is just a mental imprint to play with and keep the minds focused. The surprise comes when least expected."

"As Universal Light, Star workers work with Light Lifters in human form. In your dimension, the full demonstration called The City is a path of elevation which holds great promise and there is a light at the end of the tunnel, for the tunnel disappears as the nearing of the Holy City rings true. "

"It will not be pushed under any rug, so to speak, as it will stand as a massive live demonstration to all of the power and light of this Holy Creator, thus making this planet a place of safety and love long past due."

"The triggering of the City of Light's impact will change lives within a split second to then experience the true feeling of love. As has been said before, we play not games here. For too long warring forces have ruled and that ruling now comes to an end! No one on this planet can stop this demonstration for any reason. Since this has been centuries of slow progress, it is now being speeded up and is currently in action, for this City of Healing Technology is vastly beyond what is being currently used."

"The Sedona, Arizona area is the chosen location of impact, due to the energy fields, vortexes, star location, etc. The time is now!"

"It has been repeated from many people that from the universe come entities to take over and control us due to false advertising on the part of the ignorant, who are fearful of losing that control."

"We reply What, pray tell, is to be taken? Do people not destroy all that they can get to, from nature, animals, including humans of a different race or culture or color? Please!"

"So then awaken from your mundane daily concerns. Wash away with the strong beam of transformation light now being beamed in covering the whole earth, sucking out that which holds people into fear and concerns of the future. The light in exchange brings forth what this planet was designed for in the first place."

"You want peace on earth? You will have it! "

"Note: The world you live in on planet Earth will be seen as

another moon that shines in the heavens…

for it too has been so declared!"

Atherian: trans-audio thru the Genii

Beginning City of Light Plot Plan Information

"The City of Light can be expected to demonstrate, as has been predicted previously, with nothing that can prevent it from appearing. It is noticed that people may not always see this event as one that would demonstrate in your third dimension, only as a vision as if in an altered state of awareness."

"Each person sees an extension of him or herself, who may or may not coincide with what the Genii, has spoken of, and this is natural. However, the Genii has been chosen as an Emissary Light Spokesperson elevating the minds to regard this apparition (appearing in a third dimension level) as much as you see today, for she works all levels."

"How many times did the Dr. Bill want to quit the drawings, for his belief challenged him that such articulate plans would not be possible to build? He had to really stretch his mind to accept that a City of Light could come forth and people could physically walk into what he was being told to draw and he had no prior talent in that direction."

"These drawings with information were far beyond what he could imagine happening; yet he pursued unto the end while challenging his mental sanity. He really had to trust the inner guidance (that he taught others about) during the years of City drawings and information that came forth behind closed doors."

"To speak out now is what the Genii is being advised to do, after years of being told to keep it secret except for her 4 Keys to Light (Ancient Teachings for a Modern Age) students being Light linked during the session, opening a new corridor into the body power centers. Is this all a dream? An illusion? Yes, and so is the Great Pyramid and the homes you live in, including the trees and flowers. It would be called a "Holo-deck", a distinct part of a Hologram. It is just a preconceived thought in form."

"To bring everyone up to the same level of Spiritual advancement is no easy task. So to do that at this point could take many more centuries to achieve what could really be done in a flash. Advanced technology encased in wisdom is preparing to birth a three-dimensional form prototype structure in the form of a City of Healing Light that no one can deny."

"This, of course, can bring many people into that knowingness in a split second of vision like the greatest illusionist ever. When a magician creates an illusion, people say, "How did he do that?""

"In regards to the City and as people catch their breath because this immaculate vision stands before them unannounced, they will say, "This has to be God in action. How did he do that? " "And the Greatest Creator of all says… BECAUSE I CAN!"" End of transmission. **So Light it Be!**

The City of Light Plot Plan

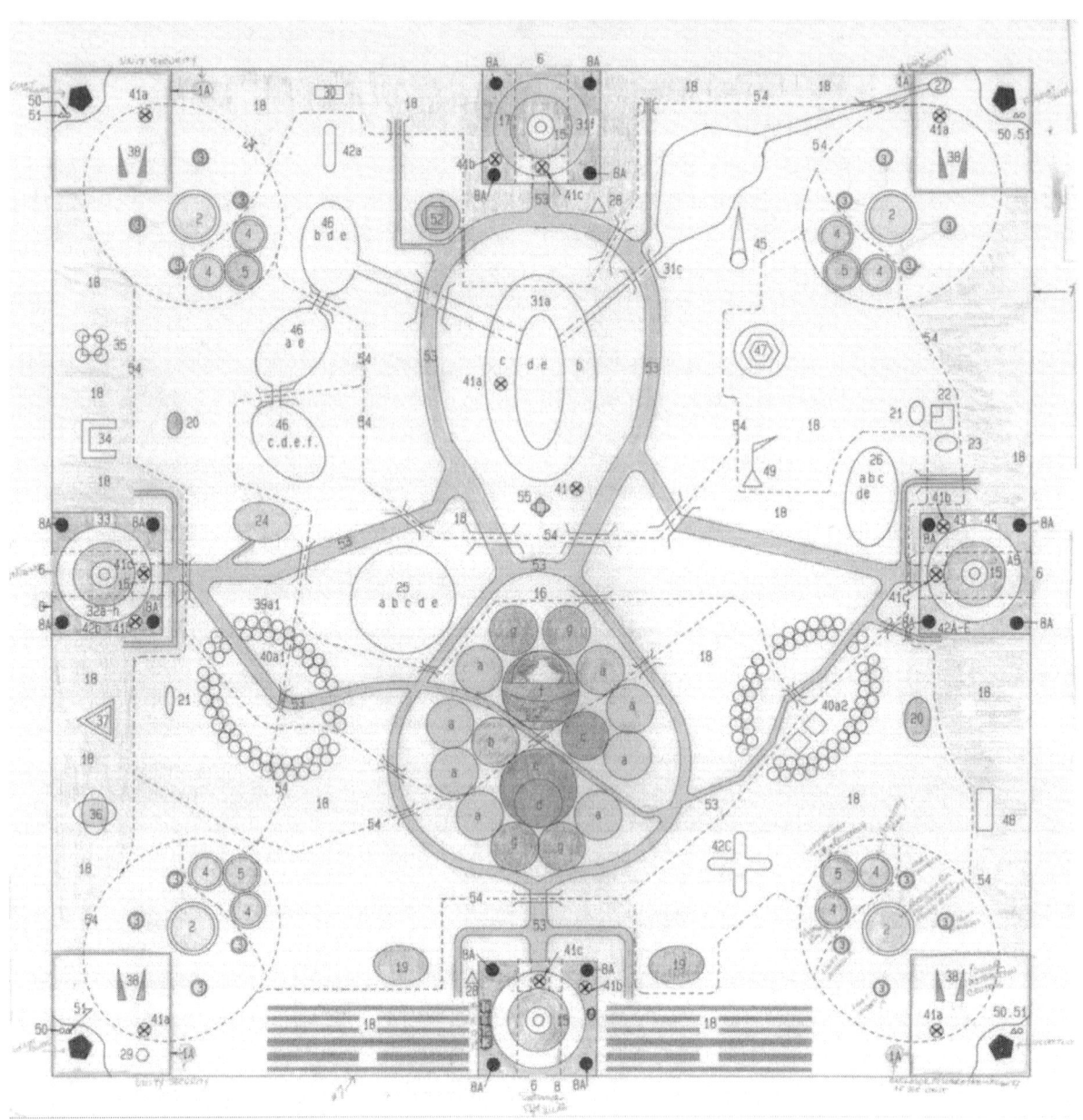

Drawing Copyright 2008 by The Light Center. All rights reserved.

The original plot plan drawn by Dr. Bill includes coded references to the transcripts that provide more detailed information on each facet of The City of Light.

Hermes, Architect of the City of Light Sedona

Hermes Trismegistus. The Master of Masters.
Thrice blessed of God!

"The mind then is not separated from God's inessentiality but united unto it, as light to sun, then in this way know God; as having all things in Himself as thoughts, the whole cosmos itself."....Hermes

Q: "Hermes, I have been told about all the areas you are proficient in and all that you created. Is it true that you were the architect of the great Pyramid and now even the City of Light?"

A: "The Hermes greets the Genii in love and the magic of the written word. Yes, this is correct and the knowing of what was to come about became a wondrous adventure. The intent of the drawn plans was to make an imprint to be deposited in the minds, although for some it would seem as a fantasy, for others as Heaven on Earth that has been spoken of so often and representative of what God has promised as Peace on Earth."

"The Sedona City of Light plot plan was sent thru the Dr. Bill as our energy fields were the same, him being my master student in the mystery school deep in the confines of the Giza Pyramid many lifetimes ago. This he did, even though it was challenging."

"Designing this heaven on earth, it was intended to be a modern up to date scientific edifice that would be more than a pretty picture in someone's mind, as it would function in healing ways not even yet attempted in your medical world for, they know not of it. The Genii has been advised of its healing powers some ages ago and has used it to great advantage."

"The coming of the City of Light Sedona has been heralded in many ways throughout the centuries. Some see it …most do not. But, as I have said 'As above …So below!' and so they will. The imprint declared itself to me as I had the light frequencies in the ecstasy of the project and, it was not to be ignored."

"This prototype City of Light was to be, for your dimensional status was needed in what you would call a 'wake-up time' even though it took many centuries in your time frame."

"You have held these sacred drawings for some time now. As you bring them forth from the archives of God's intention, you fulfill a prophecy long since hidden from the eyes of non-believers of such a planned event."

The City of Light is actually several dimensions. One you will see and three unseen as it developed thru several open corridors. This will change history forever. My pleasure in pleasing the one God was the bottom line to design this structure within a structure."

"Upon notification to the world that such a place has appeared, the energy switch takes place and that is why the 'light players' are to be in place to assist in any fear based announcements of those who have been taught to fear the wrath of God, rather than being in peace that such a gift has been delivered."

"I Hermes, stand with you as you move forward in light as light declaring wittiness to the City of Light Sedona, the beginning Healing prototype of many cities already in process awaiting the first City of Light to be demonstrated in the sacred Sedona area. We shall talk more."

"In honor of service, I am Hermes . . . Sedona City of Light Guide of the Genii. So Light it Be!"

"In the time of the coming demonstration, the City Plot Plan would have to have some recognition of something that was extraordinary, but also a bit practical in its design for people like to be comfortable in surroundings that are just that, comfortable, pleasing to the senses and the healing factor not to be ignored yet, if it was to be direct from God it would have to be magnificent in its scope and so it is all this...and more."

"So in the original design along with the scientific technology of the Great Towers and Gates, I inserted patient and family housing and eating establishments, parks of natural beauty as well as establishments of advanced teaching and even a gathering place that will hold many for various events.

What is different are, the glorified structures that are elegant beyond belief. A futuristic resort, retreat for the senses."

"You are still in human form and the basic reason for what would be seen as heaven on earth. However no Retreat Center has ever been built like this one for you do not have the materials on your planet to build it. What was once a dream is now a reality like no other dream and God did it out of its own Imagination. Imagine That!"

"Enjoy and get healed and this planet will shine in the heavens like another bright star to wish upon. So Light it be! Hermes at your service."

Importance of the City of Light High Towers and Gate Towers

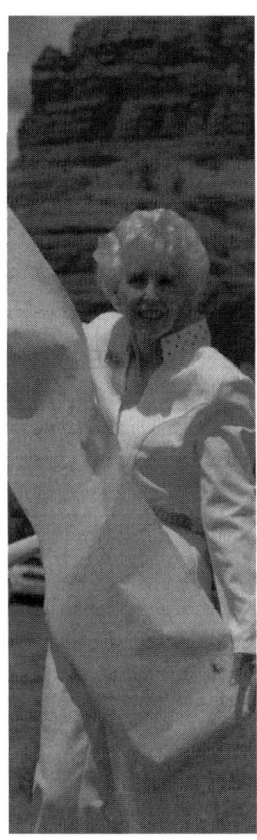

After over 25 years of maintaining faithful stewardship over the plans and architectural drawings for the City Of Light entrusted to her by her late husband, Rev. William Townsend, Genii Townsend, Co-founder of The Light Center has been led to announce the coming forth of the City of Light.

The City of Light is described in the Proclamation given to her by Light Intelligences. In the photo taken in front of Bell Rock in Sedona, Genii holds the plans for one of the four High Towers included in the plans for the City of Light.

"This is difficult to explain in your vernacular, as words can only report a portion of what now stands for progress on the way for your planet."

Genii Townsend

"**High Towers**… These four elevated stations,1,500 ft. high, (similar to a catcher's mitt) send out signals like a homing device that pull to them the Uni-phase Power Capsules (UPPC) of dynamic power not used on your planet, as it is now known to exist, although you do have different designs of energy for different reasons."

"**Gate Towers**… These structures and others within the City complex that work with the Gate Towers are complicated turbo designs. The four entrances are a welcome mat for all, as encoded in the design of the elevated five story structure is everyone's religious or spiritual belief systems, so all feel welcome like they have just found heaven on earth and all are one with no mental separation."

"The City's complex electrical systems also incorporate and work with the electro- magnetic fields to impregnate and surround this perfection-healing place of God/Spirit as only such a complex edifice could contain."

"The matrix that unfolds here is beneficial to the whole intricate embellishments contained within, around and over completely. This place of healing light is several levels in depth which can and does steer the motoring ship device, as well as the way of the healing lights of various kinds that take place"

"Nothing is left out, for in its magnificence this is a place of completion in the healing fields that your world now can only surmise as possible."

"As the City arrives (bringing the first prototype) it will supply scientists and doctors with advancing education that is superior to what is now known, for indeed you still walk with mental dinosaurs. To this point progress has been slow to non-existent."

"To intermingle, contact with others within the universe must change, and so this City of Light will do that and more. It will be as if 1,000 years of future technology has been laid at your feet within a few moments."

"The day will come when many such cities will arise on the same premise of catching the UPPCs, thus bringing energy to many places on your earth plane, but the first is the 'Attention Getter', so to speak, with the initial appearance in the Sedona, Arizona area." (See page regarding this information).

"Are the High Towers and the Gate Towers important? Oh my yes, for what is about to be deposited on your earth plane will, as has been said, be dramatic, peaceful, healing and has earth-changing advantages."

So Light it Be!

The City of Light Gate Towers

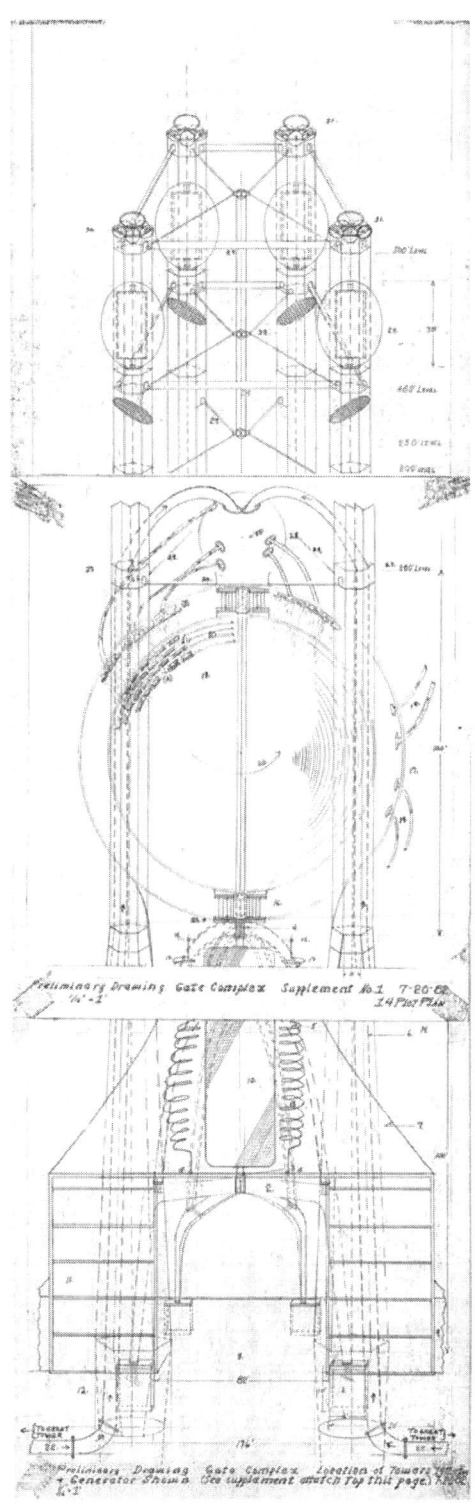

Drawing Copyright The Light Center 2008. All rights reserved.

The City of Light High Towers

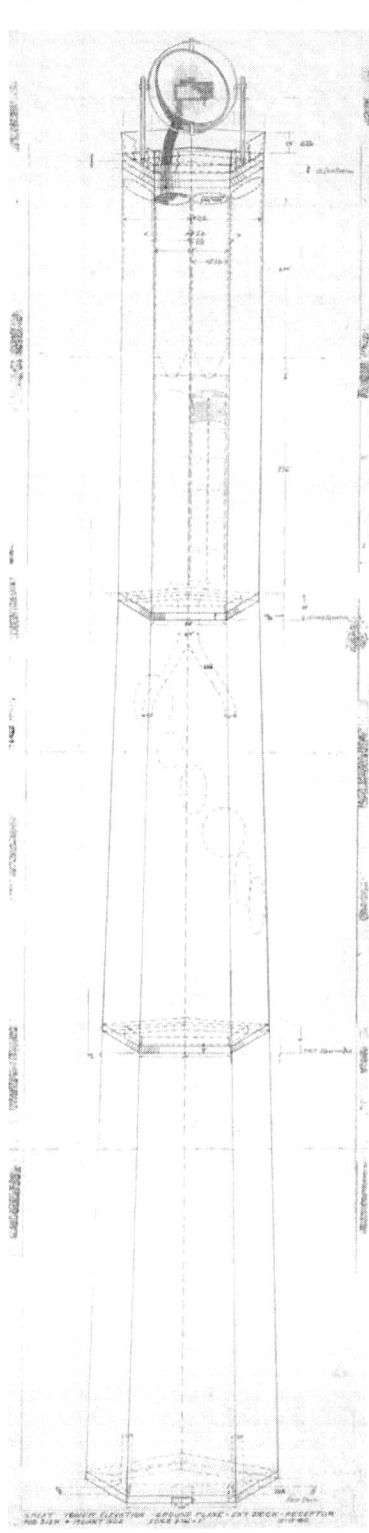

Drawing Copyright The Light Center 2008. All rights reserved.
Note: The originals drawings are several feet long.

Genii's Interior City of Light Visits

It is not easily put into words what I have seen in visions inside the interior of this place called the City of Light. Take the most grandiose words you can think of and then multiply them … a lot.

Some years ago when I was in mental conversation with my inner teachers on what they call the "All-ter-net", I asked if some day could I see inside the City before it manifested.

It took quite a few years but, indeed, I am now permitted to view some of the healing places established within its confines, and what fun this is. So this is just a small briefing just to give you an idea, for its time has come.

But first… information from one of my City Guides:

"This place of holy healing is designed to re-create the person who has the healing needed. In re-creating, this means the cells and atoms of a person's make-up are made new and thus change the whole body structure, including the mental, which is the beginning intruder anyway."

"This is done with light frequencies, most of which are not known in your field of medicine in your world. There will be no advertising needed as such, for each person is a walking healthy example of what is being said here."

"Many doctors and scientists will arrive to learn and apply as taught very advanced ways of healing yet unknown, much less tested in your world. It would be as you might call Space Technology, for that is what it is. These days you are still using methods like covered wagons when space is the perimeter to be discovered."

"Those who arrive first will learn total light healing with no surgery to cut the electrical lines. All these previous instruments of cutting and needles are barbaric at this point of advancement and will be eliminated, thus putting the patient in a calm state instead of stress where drugs are needed. New light scans will tell all."

"You, dear one, must realize that your world is in such an upheaval of change right now in preparation of this event that it will no longer be what it has been. The old world you have and are used to will have been replaced and no interest in old concepts will hold it in place. "

"You, the Genii, are experiencing this now as you set your course as a leader of the new era in process. The audio tapes you hold contain some advanced technology. The plans for the beginning formation of the City are the basic history in sound instructions with added data all for the healing comfort of those who seek, and many will find."

And so I step forth into the discovery of an invitation to glimpse for myself the greatest show on earth! On with the show; this is it!

* Stepping thru a massive five story high Gate encoded with frequencies hidden in its gold scrolling which welcomes all who want to enter into the light, the healing begins.

* Walking thru parks that have seating that gives you a loving back massage when you are seated and paths that massage your feet as you travel on them. Healing from back discomfort!

* Whatever temperature makes one comfortable it is provided, even when someone else who is next to you desires a different temperature. They, too, enjoy comfort. Can't complain here that you are hot or cold …. Healing from discomfort!

* A playing field for the big and little kids throwing and hopefully catching Light Mist balls before they disappear … Healing just by having Fun!

* The Memory Manor where unwanted memories are released in a live movie style holo-deck where pain is no longer experienced, ever from them ...Healing from released mental pain.

* The Breath-a-terium, a wonderful, unusual building that takes your old breath away and gives you in return clean breathing that is indescribable, while colors strengthen and cleanse your chakras, as well as implanting more power in its balancing light frequencies into new cells and atoms ... Respiratory Healing!

* A special pool where the water of light heals skin conditions on the spot … Wow! Healing skin irritations!

* The beginning process of the Light Modules, like a scene from Alice- in- Wonderland, walking thru a magnetized screen, harvests all your pre-medical information and DNA information without lifting pen and paper. These Light Modules are where the healing work takes the "Best of Show" award.

Thru healthy light frequencies, this place is really designed for comfort, with no knives or needles ever used. Cutting the human body light lines is not on the menu. Even the kids will enjoy this way of healing.

This is just a short indication of what to expect, and I have been blessed to be a witness inside the City of Light. It really is …

**A Healing Heaven on Earth. Imagine That!
Genii Townsend, trans-vision visitor.**

Visiting the City

Morning Message July 4, 2007

Q: "Last night I was informed that I was to go to the City of Light pre-demonstration and that it would be done in increments. What does this mean and how am I to prepare?"

A: "As the days pass the Genii will feel a strong pull to enter the City gates just to take a peek, so to speak. The vision of this will be seen and a sensing of "AH" and delight will be emotionally sensed. This would be the imprint or increment of the open passageway to the entrance."

"This will eventually make you want to see more, for the feeling and the remembrance will be of a high value, and that alone will be the incentive to want to continue to see more. This will be a pleasant offering, and the majesty of it will remain as an imprint never to be forgotten. It will seem as natural as the sun rising on a new day."

"When your system gets used to the imprint you will then be guided to take the next step, stepping farther into the City itself. The imprint will make a total believer of you, and thus a spokesperson. In your world there will be no doubt that what is to come about really exists."

Q: "Will I be able to still live and exist in this world?"

A: "Yes, but on a higher vibration, due to the electrical impulses you experience during these sessions. They will seem beyond a dream, beyond a wish, beyond imagination. This adventure is majestic. You have requested entrance, and that now is being put into place for your internal City visit. Expect to meet entities of various forms and hues, as all are part and parcel of what is bringing forth this prototype of heaven on earth called the City of Light."

Q: "What would I need to know about my preparation and how do I, in a higher state, stay functioning in my daily world?"

A: "This would sound like moving out of your current world, but on the contrary, the vibration system will be enhanced so in the frequencies in the vortexes you will become more balanced as you get equalized with the vortexes, not separate."

Q: "Traveling with the City data, how does this work?"

A: "Travel will become more important, and having a co-partner would be an advantage, if they too are frequency acceptors ready to assist and be part of this movement out to spread the word."

"Again it is to be remembered that you and the Charles are both connected on the same light strand, and this connection with people outside you can harvest a miracle of advantages, which include financial as well."

"This is not to say that the way of Light cannot bring forth the desired harvest from other areas, but as you would say, 'This is hot right now'. We say it will remain that way."

"What is being said here to travel to various locations of guided interests will touch down in places where people will begin to take notice and pay attention to this demonstration of 'City prototype' value. Just permit the days to ascend on each other, but be open to the new, for it is right here and right now."

"It is advised also that the Charles be open to his guidance in regard to what is being said here, for the mental impact of what he is into here could descend on him at any moment."

"His focus is on one area, education, and the producing of it globally; however, his main function is now being advised of the City entrance and that it would be wise counsel to begin to take a stronger look at what he is being handed by God and guided by the Christ he adores."

"These are not just daydreams of future happenings. You both are on the cutting edge of the happening. Request guidance constantly on this area, for the correct people need to be advised of the contents of what is being said here, and together travel is certainly indicated to render vocal service to others in person as well as other ways."

"The time is apparent and you are destined to be examples of what it is to be enlightened in human form by God."

Genii Experiences the City of Light – Vision Visit 1

Entering the South Gate

Question: City VISION Guidance?

Genii's Guide: "As the time collapses in your directive sensing, the Genii will relate more and more into the visions of the City interior. It will become more like a dream yet, as visits increase, very visible so much so that you will begin to feel at home rather than a visitor.

It will seem like you have been whisked away into another reality and of course that is the reality of this situation of advanced technology that is so real that no one will ever be able to say to you ever that it does not exist!"

"The elevation of your consciousness will make this possible. You have been recently to the South Gate and experienced the grandeur and luxury of its design. The gold design around the rim of the horseshoe entrance is indeed what you would call pure gold, however it is more, as it is embellished in light fragments not found on your planet."

"Its thickness which you estimate as about 3-4 inches holds within its interior mixture, the magnet of light which has the ability to make anyone about to enter, feel very welcome with no feeling of fear. One will feel a wanting to enter on ones knees in adoration for the one God who put up this adoration welcome sign."

"Each of the 4 Gates is similar in repeat. The entrance marks the beginning and as you continue your journey to the interior you will be amazed at the magnificence of what you will behold for it is God blessed and God demands the best and…gets it."

(Genii vision note) As I peeked thru the gate all I could see was lush greenery and a fragrance but could not identify the fragrance but it was very pleasant and light and made me feel I wanted to smell more. Kind of like the cartoons of a freshly baked pie with streams of drawn fragrance drifting as a come-to-me invitation.

TEACHER: "For this moment, just enjoy that thought for there is quite an adventure ahead beyond your current belief systems. God beholds beauty untold as yet, and welcomes the Genii whose heart has been here for lo these many years."

"So Light it be. We bid you the light of the eternal day in peace and love."

Part # 2 Second Visit – The Energy Park

The first thing I see as I pass through the same Gate as before, straight ahead is a park-like setting. Resting places I assume are benches yet, looking different. They seem to be alive with a relaxing vibratory of some sort within them. There is a walkway path that also seems to vibrate, making my feet feel very comfortable and walking is quite enjoyable.

The grass is shades of green from dark to light making a wavy kind of pattern on the ground that seems to rest my eyes. There are flowers but none I can identify. The colors are exquisite and the fragrances blend into an aroma that could be intoxicating as it is so relaxing.

The trees also had blossoms of some unknown kind and darting within the branches were very colorful tiny little birds also indefinable. They did not chirp but had a humming sound that made me feel that nothing else mattered. I was at home. It looks like a very large park and I can see a small waterfall nearby that has pink water. Maybe it has a light under it.

There is an unseen frequency that has been felt as soon as I entered which quite balanced my nervous system. I just wandered alone for a bit. Over-hanging trees like willows covered whatever was beyond it.

I have a sudden sensing that a City Guide will soon join me, "Is this correct?"

Teacher (voice): "The Genii will indeed be introduced to an exceptional scientific guide who will escort you thru the City of Light to the point that you be so attuned that it will be seen and felt as the City of Love."

"You are welcomed into the interior not as a visitor, but as a friend of the Light Beings who reside here that are part of making this City the Light that it is. Welcome…enjoy your Vision."

"We bid you the light of the Eternal day in peace and in love…Now!"

Part # 3 Third Visit – Meeting with My City Guide

As I stepped closer to the beautiful fragrant trees before me that blocked my view, I found I didn't have to move an inch, for stepping thru them like a performer moving gracefully onto a stage, stepped a light in human form.

He was indeed a vision. A cross between Sean Connery and someone not of this local world like Star Wars Obi -Wan and that sensing was prevalent and whatever it was, it had served him well.

"Be not afraid" was his opening introduction as he held out his hand in friendship smiling as he took mine. As he did a jolt of energy went through me like an electric shot of something feeling really good.

"I am pleased to meet you," I stammered slightly. He laughed as his short silver beard glistened in the light.

"Would it not be a good idea for you since this City of Light is part of your destiny to join me in a tour? I can assure you that it will be tantalizing and refreshingly informative and not to forget healing."

"'Of course, thanks. As a beginning what would I call you? What is your name I mean?"

"You may refer to me as LaLuke, destiny provider of City information, visions and delightful experiences" and as he smiled said, "I promise you that I will take very good care of you."

With that he parted the leafy trees and I stepped through. I could hardly believe what I was seeing and feeling. It was awesome, beautiful and even the air tasted good.

Indeed like LaLuke promised, looks like I am being delightfully taken care of. Wow! I think I will really enjoy being this girl.

Thanks God for this magnificent visit.

City Interior Visit- The Reflection of a New Beginning

And the gates of inner-spection open once more for the Genii to be guided in vision. Meeting with my city guide LaLuke, I see in front of us a short stoned path camouflaged by flowing type willow trees with tiny pink flowers and the fragrance was intoxicating.

They hung low and as we moved them aside like curtains on a stage, we found ourselves facing unusual Star Trek buildings of several designs all white and sparkly. They surrounded a fountain that poured something that released bubbles.

It was then that I noticed a lady-like entity who stood beside it and she smiled at us as we moved near her. She didn't say anything but motioned me to look into this bubbly pool. Now what could this be, another healing pool?

"Of course" came an unseen voice. I looked over the edge and the reflection I saw was one of youthful delight. All else had disappeared and I saw a newborn baby...was this me?

"In a way" said my Guide. This is the human reflection of the new you being newly born. When one looks into this pool (which is a mirror of past, present, and now future) you can see where you have been and are now re-born into the visual realization of that."

"Someone else would see a teen, someone else, an aged person. It is how you see yourself in this mirror of life. You have been on the spiritual path for a while, and are ready to be new born and so, the reflection equals that image. Each previous step you have taken in life has dropped off like a cloak of darkness and you began to get lighter as you moved through various trials and tribulations."

"You might call it a makeover in your current vocabulary. In your world validation is needed to constantly reinforce your spiritual path. In this world is validation of turmoil and change. So this new baby is the new you, who looks upon this world through new eyes ready to accept her place."

I looked again into this pool of reflection and I smiled for the baby I saw was blowing bubbles that floated into the clear air.

"How would this pool heal someone?" I asked

"This is a reflection of where someone is now. It tells a vision story. Some people have a way to go for some see themselves as various mental stages from young to old."

"No matter what they may think topside so to speak, subconsciously is what comes to the surface and they can see it. One cannot change what they do not recognize of themselves so this reflective mirror does that for them. A road map if you will on the way to Illumination."

"Now that you have seen the re-born, you can know that the past concerns and worries have no place for, you are re-born and know not of such things."

"How do I explain this on my City tour to others?"

Smiling my Guide said," The fun of the City of Light is that it in-lightens at special locations in the city interior. This would be a checkpoint if you will of validation. Another check point would have your thoughts manifest, and seeing your thoughts could make for a change, for as on a computer you can see what you are thinking at any given moment of time and when some thoughts that are repeated over and over they can look very tiresome and so they are released, then that is that!"

"The checkpoints throughout the City give notice of who and where you are on any given moment and sometime others can see them too for if they were flashed on a large enough screen for all to see, what would you do to change your thinking? Elevation of thoughts induces clearer thinking."

And with this he led me back to the gate. I thanked him and looking up I see a sign that says" You are welcome."

This City of Light is not only healing, but magic as well…

We are to be pleasantly blessed.

Hmmm …newborn in light… how God is this!

City of Light Tour – The Fountain of Light

Q: Please describe the City fountain in the center of the City grounds and its properties.

"First of all there is one. It stands approximately 15 feet high from the base which itself is on a pedestal of approximately 3 feet high."

"This magnificent structure has a velocity of frequencies that permit the fountain to have healing powers (to a certain extent) and attracting those who are near the base, the uplifting of their mental (which in itself lifts the physical systems.)"

"The light that is emitted from it is controlled by the underground surveillance technicians who have themselves had such a raising of consciousness that is beyond your local thinking. (It is known to the Genii that a complete underground City itself lies beneath the property.) The base of the fountain carries the electrical circuitry that promotes the uplifting properties that affect all who are near."

"The base or the bowl of the Fountain can be seen as large flower petals. Each one emanates colored lights like rolling waves of prismatic rainbows. There are four large petals facing the four cardinal points north, south, east and west. It is a light modular in action."

"From the center, like the pistils of a flower, light extends 15 more feet into the air spilling down on those who may be seated or standing nearby."

"The moods and attitudes then would change for the better as the frequencies connect with each person's electrical system. Indeed this Fountain is to be enjoyed in awe and happiness as they experience it in its intensity."

"This then is just the beginning point of your current mental projection into the City of Light. Those involved in this outer process now being spoken of are admonished not to share this information with others not involved in this process. It is to remain only in your mind for viewing with your guide."

"Daily devotional work with the tonal –vision will not only bring it into your view mentally but through this singular process can bring it into view for the masses."

"You are encouraged to direct your viewing daily within yourself and feel what this Fountain of Light can really do for yourself while mentally in its proximity."

"You with the others involved have the combined power to bring forth the City into manifestation."

"This then is the beginning of the beginning. It is sacred and modern beyond belief. It is scientifically modern beyond belief."

"It is now a part of your life's path should you choose to accept this blessed offering to assist in the process."

"Welcome to the City of Light….

First in your mind,

Then in your heart,

Then on the planet for all to see."

"God is, I am, The City and I are one! So Light it Be!"

Trans-audio medium Genii Townsend

Filling In the Blanks

I felt this morning to re-enter the City of Light for my next vision visit.... As I re-enter through what seems to be the same gate I did before I see several entities smiling and pointing me to a path different than the one I was previously on.

Ahead I see my City Guide La-Luke who smiles as I near him. He beckons me to sit with him on an interesting type of bench that has the ability to massage the body as well. There are lots of flowers and I hear birds chirping someplace unseen. It is like being in a glass bubble.

It is all quite pleasant, and comfortable. His energy field is very relaxing and loving. I wanted to ask him some questions.

Genii: "Tell me more about this City of Healing Light."

He smiled and replied, "Indeed, this place of Holy Healing is designed to 're-create' the person who needs the healing. In recreating, this means the cells and atoms of that person's make-up are reproduced new and thus changes the whole body structure including the mental, which is the beginning intruder anyway."

"This of course is done with light frequencies, most of which are not known in your fields of medicine in your world. I have shown you so far, examples of the healing delight, people will find here. There will be no advertising needed as such you have today as each person is a walking healthy example of what is being said here."

"Many doctors and scientists will arrive to learn and apply as taught of this very advanced way of healing yet unknown much less tested. It would be as you might call 'space technology' for that is what it is. These days you are still using ideas and methods like a covered wagon when space is the perimeter to be discovered."

"Those who arrive first will learn total light healing with no surgery to cut the electrical lines within the body. All these previous instruments

of cutting and with needles are barbaric at this point of advancement and will be eliminated, thus putting the patient in a calm state instead of stress where drugs are needed. New Light scans will tell all."

"What is being used now will be obsolete and one will look back at it like an old wagon train crossing the desert. Light changes will take place daily."

G: "What will be the response of the people when the City of Light appears?"

L-L "Varied, everything from pre-programmed fear to adoration that the Christ has reappeared and there is peace on earth. We have been saved. Praise God!"

"The Planet's governments will be highly suspicious after being programmed to immediately interfere with anything suspicious and unusual and this certainly is that for it cannot be denied. It is all plain to see."

G: "How can I be of service?"

L-L: "Actually you already are and being programmed even further to be a spokesperson among many who sense something is forming or coming but may not know what yet. Some who do, do not speak of it yet lest the negativity enter and disturb."

G: "Will babies be born in the City and how would that affect their life?"

L-L: "To answer the first part, yes they will be and most mothers would be honored to have such an experience of her child being born in light, as light, and through light, which would of course permit them to be walking, talking, living light personages that will change what would need changing."

"You must realize that your world is in such an upheaval of change right now in preparation of this event that it will no longer be what it has been. The old world you have and are used to will have been replaced and no interest in history would take its place and no old concepts will hold the past in place."

"What you Genii are experiencing right now is a very lesser degree of upheaval as we set your course as a leader of the new era in process. The audio tapes you hold contain some advanced technology and the beginning formation of the City plans are the basic history of the development of the City in sound instructions."

"What is now being shown you here begins to fill in the blanks, the empty spaces, with added data all for the healing comfort of those who seek and many will find."

"You have noticed that many people are leaving your planet through your death process as every being is being amped up and it can get very strong if one is unwilling to change with it."

"Now then, (and he stood up) we shall continue our tour on your next visit. For now feel the vibration level here and take that back with you for you will be called on soon again to reveal the City of Light."

"Blessings dear one… I love you."

And with that in a blaze of light he was gone leaving me with the awe of this whole experience, a Holy one to be sure. I am blessed that each visit gives me one more clue of what is to come about…ready or not.

So Light it be!

The Empowerment Emporium

June 22, 2008

Once again, having been guided to re-enter through inner vision, I pass through the south Gate, thus meeting my City Guide, LaLuke. He smiles as he takes my hand and we walk forward. As I glance at the Gate Towers all shiny and beautiful, I wondered at the holy majesty of these enormous structures that loom so huge above me, giving off a feeling of such peace as I have never experienced.

The outside world of turmoil had disappeared and as he led me forward I was in awe. One could not be otherwise.

LaLuke walked me through the park of the Relaxation Massage Benches to yet another path of exploration.We walked to a garden-type lattice-covered tunnel that smelled heavenly, with tiny white blossoms reaching out to give one much sensual pleasure.

As we came to the end, there in front of us was a white building with golden spires that were several stories high. At the doorway in welcome were two semi-transparent entities that I refer to as see-throughs. They assisted in this spirit/human experience.

Since this City is a Healing place, I expected to see more ways of healing the physical and mental bodies we walk around in. Interestingly, as we stepped inside, the floor seemed to move gently like it had a life of its own.

Genii: "Where are we?"

LaLuke: "What see you?"

G: I looked around as faint colors floated in the air. Emotional balance was experienced even with the floor moving gently.

LL: "This is an Emotional Balancing Building. You use the word "emporium". This could be considered an Emotional Emporium.

As each person enters, the colors that that person needs are attached to them. This is to verify that his power centers are balanced."

"Remember what was told you eons ago of the colors/fragrances/ etcetera of each of the body power centers? Here one can experience this. As the colors and lights activate the body senses, they can give a major report of those functions, and they can be experienced in this City."

So here it was, gentle movement of the floor massaging the feet (for we had left our shoes outside) and beautiful colors floated around us inviting us to accept the balancing of these Power Center chakras.

In this building if anything was not functioning energy-wise it was put to rest, for in balancing one felt euphoric and totally healthy.

I recognized from the first writings of the City by Dr. B. there were very many regular places we, as humans, would recognize. This seems to be the covering of all that, like filling in the blanks that were unseen but were there all the time.

The balancing tunnel brought out the best of me, since I now felt balanced. I should add that inside screens of some sort showed which chakras needed the balancing and the colors changed to permit this to happen. So then it was a carousel of color that balanced the power centers, thus lifting the person's emotional and spirit senses to a heightened degree and a feeling of happiness and joy was experienced, including being totally relaxed.

One could also take a mental area (of any different concern) to be washed out in this emotional emporium. Thus, be it love needed, that chakra now felt that. If fear release was desired, that, too, was completed. Any mental area was taken care of due to the indoctrination beginning with this covered building of rainbow lights.

If one had a worry when they went in and through this building, it was cleared out from the subconscious. It was amazing to see and feel the power centers being cleared.

The Emotional Empowerment Emporium was ready, then, to be entered into, and after we exited the flower-covered bridge-like exterior, we entered in the emporium itself, where in a circular mall-type setting where there were many spaces or rooms which were open to give what that person now desired with no reservations.

If one desired more love, they stepped inside and got it through feeling and heart. If one desired more fun, another room provided that, et cetera, et cetera. Wishes were granted.

The emotional charges of unbalance were not sensed any longer. You literally came out a happy, balanced person.

Well, Joy to the World! The Lord (City) has come. The unbalanced is Light balanced and being lifted in emotion far enough to empower others.

Emporium Empowerment – How great is this?

Very!

Visit to the City of Light Birth-aterium

May 16, 2008

Genii: "I sense a return to the City of Light again. What am I to see?" and with this I saw the following impression......

And the beauty of the interior brings my breath to a momentary halt as we would say 'breath-taking'. But it is even beyond that for the breath of what we may call God does emanate here. It is as simple as that, yet mind-changing in its value.

I may never be the same again in my daily world. I see a path of steps that seem lit and make a tinkling sound-feeling as I step on them one at a time. My City Guide La Luke smiles and leads me on the "Toning Stones."

We walk across a small bridge where tiny fish that look like dolphins leap out and then duck under in play. I was busy enjoying them and he motioned me to look up and in doing that a large building was fairly near circular in design, and with a door you could (it seemed) melt through. And we did. It was kind of like Jell-O with no flavor. What? Oh well. This is really getting sci-fi.

The interior was like a very big center hotel lobby with plants and flowers and water falling into various pools where swans swam and the whole area was lit from the skylight opening. There were women dressed in pastel rainbow colors of sheers in attendance who smiled at us. What's not to smile about here? Wondering what this was and where we were going, I suddenly asked LaLuke where we were.

LaLuke: "We are in the Birth-atrium." he replied.

Genii: "Is this like the Breath-atrium?"

LaLike : "Not quite but breathing is important." he smiled. "This is where new Earthlings are born."

Genii: "Now I am really getting interested."

LaLuke: "They are toned and breathed into being. Come I will show you."

We walked into a corridor leading away from this beautiful center so clean and filled with the aroma of spring flowers in bloom, then we took a slight turn and up a few steps to a viewing center to look down into the birthing 'pod' as it was referred to.

Three ladies were in a natural birthing process. Like in the Light modules they lay on floatation beds. The Pod light was mesmerizing in its soft brilliance, and it was quickly seen that other than the birthing mother, women attendants dressed in white, and this soft light which seemed to come from the women's auras, nothing else was seen.

No hospital paraphernalia anywhere and, this was a peaceful place of total joy. No screaming, telling to push, or pushing, no profanity or any of the hard labor we go through. It was delightfully amazing and what a surprise to witness this new beginning. The babies were born in light and love and just floated out into this world laughing and gurgling. The mothers were having a "birthing party", imagine that! The babies were born being happy to be here and take their first breath.

As each baby was delivered a different sound was heard. Each one had their own tone. I watched the colored auras around the attendants change as each baby arrived. This indeed was the way babies should be able to come into the world easily and effortless and with no physical problems. Just pure and happy to be here. This must be the way we are supposed to be born! Praise God...we need this City of Light!

My Guide told me that pre-breathing exercises are addressed before they enter here and in the birth canal, the baby picks up this breath frequency and the indwelling tone becomes the harmony that resides within each child upon birth.

This is the best way of giving birth to children who will make up our new world. As more Light Cities appear the pre-mothers will have new and different things to do that will change their DNA for, the fetus that is the child, of the future are truly little Light Beings in every sense of the word.

Genii: "This is truly God in light healing."

LaLuke: "Interesting with this way of birthing, there is no healing to be done. This is where your physicians will be able to learn new and sensible ways to remove the old unreliable ones of guess work and the doctors will not have to search for answers they will just inwardly know, and will be correct".

"Many doctors and scientists will come for advanced light teaching such as maybe your friend doctor Miller and be invited to be one of those who will want to know more of Light Techniques used here...So now we leave."

He turned around as I took one more glance and feeling of this birthing place where love and the light that beckons the new babies to be born... loved and free!

So Light it Be!

The Deciding Place

July 27, 2008

I just could not resist the inner invitation to travel back into the City of Light interior this morning, so in my quiet time I laid aside my usual meditation practices to watch whatever was to be presented, fully knowing I haven't a clue what that will be. So with a sip of my morning tea here I go . . .

Closing my eyes but still being open to anything, I find myself again standing in front of one of the massive 5 stories tall great Gate Towers. It is so extremely beautiful it could, as we say, take your breath away. The scene was enhanced with the sun reflecting it in all directions.

I stand alone and I can see a bit into the interior that I had visited before, the park with the bench type seating that massages your body, sending shivers of feeling-good vibes.

No sound was detected, but a few brightly-colored birds darted from branch to branch in willow-type trees, as flowers of all descriptions swayed merrily on their stems. I sat here getting massaged, while seeing this amazing place. I wondered if I was like Dorothy and had made it over the rainbow. .

As my eyes were closed on this Sunday morning blocking out the Sedona sunshine, I just let the scene develop into what it was supposed to contain. I felt a presence near me and my city guide, La-Luke, was there smiling. "Relaxing, are you?" he inquired.

Genii: "Yes. I can do nothing else but wonder what I did to deserve being able to be in this holy place. Feeling good can take place so quickly here." I replied.

LaLuke: "The interior has many techniques of healing, for it is a facility designed to do that. If people on this planet were all healed there would be no need for the City at all, but centuries of conflict have produced a high volume of healings needed. Come, we will walk a bit and start at the beginning." He took my hand and I felt a whole lot of energy connecting to me.

We began to walk what I sensed was some sort of Labyrinth of Light. We walked through the willow trees and past the Healing Fountain Pool that healed Skin Abrasions. I remember putting a finger into the strange, thick water and sensing something was taking place, even though I had no problem with the finger. Just being near, my skin felt refreshed, and the dry skin cream I used in my earth world was, indeed, not needed here.

Looking around the many buildings newly seen led me to believe that this place is huge and it could go on for miles. I guessed that each one could do different kinds of healings. "Quite so," said my guide, reading my thoughts telepathically.

LaLuke: "In order to heal the human body through the mental path of human thought, that human, in his mental capacity, has to believe that it is fact, not fiction, because the belief system is connected to the emotional tract. The building they are entering is, indeed, the one that can cure what ails them. Know that if you humans go into that place, you are assured that you will be healed of ...whatever is important."

"Many buildings are designed to serve one area of healing only. Within the healing properties of this or that building comes the Advanced Light Technology, far beyond what is reached at this point in your medical advancement, as good as it is learning to be. It just was taking so long to bring it all forth that it was decided to bring forth the City to be the prototype of advancement. This you already have been advised, so now we shall enter the building on your right."

This building was white, sort of round with spirals like a unicorn horn heading skyward. White and gold seem to be the chosen colors of the buildings so far.

"This building is THE DECIDING PLACE, the beginning location of service where one decides what ailment needs attention that would satisfy their mind. Be it mental, spiritual, emotional or whatever, all are attached to the physical body temple. In this place the discernment of the person decides what should be taken care of."

Inside the building was like several others, with a center circular lobby-type setting where, again, the beauty of a gently flowing pool relaxed me totally. Looking around I see several horseshoe-shaped openings leading to corridors with windowed rooms that have no one inside, just lights, One room had pink lights, another blue, et cetera. The colors vary from darker to almost invisible lightness.

Genii: "What is this?" I asked.

LaLuke: "Each room varies due to the person inside. As the colors emanate, the one that is applied is not only their favorite color but one that is compatible with their light body. Here is where the decisions are made to continue the process of total healing. It is high technology, but also what you can simply understand at your level of understanding. So then this is the Building of Decision, and the healing has already begun. But now it is time to take you back to the Gate, for you have had enough light levels now and you have to function in your physical world."

All this is breathtaking to be sure, to the point of almost non belief, but believe you me I am truly a believer ... thanks, God, for the invitation. This is indeed God's favor activated.

So Light it be!

The Institute of Image Imprinting

Another City of Light Visit August 4, 2008

Unexpectedly I was delivered this invision information, viewing a large white circular-front building with a gold circular dome. Inside there were many, many rooms. Each room could hold only one to two persons, the viewer and n assistant guide as desired. These were called Personal Viewing Rooms.

When a person comes in, they face a big screen of some sort. They now have, or previously had, made a decision on what their desire or wish is that they want to see completed. They can see what they are thinking about at any given split second moment of time. The guide is there to assist but not interfere with the decision-making.

The person sits down, closes their eyes, pulls up the desire mentally and then opens their eyes and watches the screen for, the desire is on the screen, in full view. The mind in its fluctuation quickly can come and alter or switch that desire and that is also seen. The mind does much switching due to the right and left brain input.

In other words they are watching their own thoughts right before them, and how the mind can make changes in a split second thus changing the beginning power level of that desire. Even the feelings are recorded as well as colors etc.

This can continue until the person has the original desire or wish implanted into the perfect image desired for when that is done the perfection is established and the final demonstration is produced in their world.

Note: The Institute of Image Imprint is secure in the knowledge that this futuristic programming will be hailed as the best technology of the century for, the imagination of desire has laid the ground work and achieved the results thus, making a dream wish desired come true in their eyes.

Trans-audio vision...Genii

The Star Wings of a Healing Building

Inner City Visit July 8, 2008

QUESTION: (To my guides) "And what would be my adventure tonight? Anyone want a conversation?"

ANSWER: "Yes, several are in attendance."

QUESTION: "Okay. What shall we talk about?"

ANSWER: "That which is always interesting."

QUESTION: "The City?"

ANSWER: "Of course. Permit you to travel again beyond the gates and follow a new path that leads to yet another healing location."

A VISIT TO THE INNER CITY

I then find my vision self at a new location looking at a huge building that has five star- shaped points. The building is silver and is reminiscent of a cosmic sci-fi type.

Each point is a laboratory where different light techniques are tested and finalized.

QUESTION: "How many light ways are there to heal with?"

ANSWER: "As many as the healings that are needed, for various people have on your planet mental imprints that suggest a healing is desired. Your hospitals and doctors' offices are overrun with appearances needing attention, so each of the Star Wings introduce the advancement and the best in cosmic technology beyond your current situations. Come, we take a peek into one."

We entered the building center filled with such fresh air as I have never experienced before, and not from air conditioners it seems. Each Star Wing protruded from this center point. We headed for one wing and passed thru a DNA screen like in the light modules but yet different.

In doing so, Light Technicians can see in advance what may be a new malady appearing which will again be added into the advanced technology, thus stopping it before it has a chance to disrupt the light body functions of the person. Amazing! They were making something out of nothing.

What they were doing was unclear to me. All I could see was glowing particles and then see how they magically went together like pieces of a puzzle. The Light Technicians were like "see-throughs" to me, but I could see them clearly.

If this is all E.T. stuff, they are very welcome and desired by yours truly. No one there said anything, but I did catch a smile now and then.

"What is happening here?" I say, having a great time viewing the unknown.

The answer is, "Magic in the making. You say you like magic? Well, dear student, this is it!"

(At this point there was an interruption in the house and the vision stopped, but I was pleased to see this Star Trek way of bringing forth what is unknown ... yet with good times ahead.)

So Light It Be!

The Playing Field

January 2, 2008

Having taken the first vision visits into the City interior I am advised to return, and I do just that …

Traveling clockwise with my Guide La-Luke, we follow a wide path where yet another park-like area is noted. This one is different because it has a shimmer and children "'see through" entities are playing by throwing small balls of light and laughing as the balls disappear in a layer of some kind of mist hanging low overhead. The balls were made from this shimmering mist. What was going on?

My guide smiled and said that this shimmering mist was just another type of light. This was why the children were laughing, for it made them feel so good that they could do nothing else but to watch the light balls disappear like melted snow balls, which made it all the funnier.

He requested I try one.

I reached up into this lower layer of strange mist and grabbed a handful of light stuff. It felt of no weight, just like nothing, but my hands were guided to make a ball, so I did. It was like making something out of nothing, which I guess we do when we create from an unseen thought into a full-fledged creation of some sort. However, it was very strange!

I threw it at La-Luke but it disappeared into the mist again before it got to him. I asked him if this had to do with healing?

He reported, "Of course! The Fun Balls of Misty Light make those playing feel good, and when you feel good, the cells in the body/mind connection heal … simple analogy!"

And with that he nudges me to move with him on our continued path in the City of light.

Note: What fun to have fun with the unexpected! This is quite a place, where even fun heals. We all knew that didn't we, or did we?

Healing the Future through the City of Light

Morning Message July 6, 2008

Q: Please expand on the healing properties of the City for families and children as well.

A: "Healing facilities of many kinds are available, and even the most wounded on any level can find a peaceful solution. Light technicians working with those who seek healings, advice, and directions can find it there. Those professionals like the Kathie Brodie who works with the hypnotherapy area can import her knowledge but at a higher level due to the energy frequencies developed within the City structure."

"What you refer to as natural healing induced by the energy fields of the City can bring immediate response to those seeking a healing. The Genii has visited several such places where this is apparent. Children can be a quick study for healing as they are more open to receive, but even the adults' pre-programming gets altered under such circumstances. Again, all is achieved by light."

THE LIGHT MODULES

"The Genii observes the patients under-glowing in treatment of various lights via the inner vision technique, for whatever the person's needs may be now. Upon arrival it this location, instead of going through much paperwork on the past ailments, etc. of that patient, they merely walk through an EPS (Electronic Portal Screen) entrance, at which time all the imprints of the DNA information, which are in a coded form, are instantly picked up by the Light Technician for healing action while the patient reclines on a floatation bed held in an electromagnetic field. All this works well with the light body of the person seeking help."

"The Light Modules themselves are a scientific wonder to experience, from the unseen fragrances to the unusual musical healing tones and replenishing pleasant moments of relaxation. From simple opening releasing for introductory light surgery (where no knives, etc. are used), to the birthing of a newborn in the Birth-a-terium, this indeed is a healing location like no other ever witnessed and it is why the City of Light is so named."

Why a City?

"City represents a large location, community of many people, and the attraction of the healing facilities which make for an unusual place to get the mental, physical, emotional and spiritual together to be healed and all at the same time due to various unusual ways, while in this awesome beauty. Even a bit of fun is enjoyed when in a golf course normality.

Players play with gold balls, which is uplifting when this ball of energy always goes to the correct location. Expect some normal locations, but in the finery that only God could develop."

"Those who have negative feelings outside the Great Gates, they will begin to dissipate as they enter the City inside in welcome. Expect the unexpected to enjoy and heal no matter what the individual situation, for indeed this is a healing heaven on earth."

"So then continue to delight in what is to come about, for mankind, like no other, will see a magnificent City of Light and all it contains, as the greatest show on earth settles down as a major cosmic event never experienced before."

So Light it Be!

UFO Visitors

November 12, 2007

Q: Genii : "I watched Larry King's show the other day when I heard that today in Washington D.C. a meeting is to be held there with people from 8 different countries confirming that they have witnessed UFO's and that finally attention is to be given it. What can be told me of this meeting?"

A:" The Genii senses joyfully that this news is a blessing and long past due. Those who begin to speak out will attract more that is yet hidden by those who have seen but are afraid to speak out."

"Now the energy intrudes into the darkness of minds. Those of us who venture into your dimension give just enough credence of appearance and delight in the controversy that is to take place."

"As each one speaks, it lays the ground work for others to join in and say, Yes, there are visitors of some kind from other places and we on planet earth are not alone but, maybe in the hearts of supporting friends."

"THERE IS NOTHING TO TAKE-OVER HERE. The films with a few exceptions put on a sad light on what actually is a support and not a take-over situation of destruction. You do that very well yourselves. This comes from minds that hold fear as a 'God other' and out of mental control in that position. Such nonsense!"

"Benevolent beings of Light Intelligence have been supporting for eons of time and the destruction of your planet now takes the minds to finally say 'It is time to look at what we have done'."

"Nature in revolt now steps up to also get attention, for this blessed planet deserves to join others as the cosmos of intelligence serves as a teacher. So we watch and see what takes place on the government ground as people of note speak out their views. . . we shall see."

"All is in pre-preparation of the City of Light to manifest and we are pleased to be contributors of advanced thinking. Pay attention, there is more coming and Peace will reign one way or another."

UFOs and The City of Light

Morning Message April 22, 2008

Q: "Once more the television is reporting UFO Light sightings over Phoenix AZ, (that are now becoming famous.) What can be said of this phenomenon, and does it have anything to do with the City of Light coming forth?"

A: "Yes, absolutely! These light ships are shown periodically, only to show that there is something beyond this planet that is alive and has intelligence far beyond what appears here as human, thus giving the searching minds something to ponder on besides themselves, which it normally has to do to survive."

"The lights of the so called UFOs are just that, lights of UFOs bringing forth those of higher intelligence supporting the manifestations coming forth as the City of Light. Were you shown the gold ships on the roofs of buildings in the interior of the City visit? Of course. When stepping into one on the tops of the buildings called the Breath-atrium did you not observe many more like them? Of course."

"The human factor of this planet is still in the dinosaur stage of development, and some believe war is the answer ... please! Although some stages of learning are now being propelled swiftly, it has been and is slow, and the planet suffers as a result under ignorant thinking. Those who come bring not only Intelligence but energy vibrations that are propelling the healing of this planet, which for you humans have to come from the mind and still too many are in an ego-ignorant stage. While many teachers are recognizing changes are important they, too, may need some adjustments into higher thinking."

"As the space vehicles show themselves periodically in the heavens, this is preparation, so to speak. Does the Genii have intelligence teachers of high space considered E.T.s? Of course! Do the Sedona/Phoenix and surrounding areas have extraordinary energy pulls due to the vortexes and underground grid lines of light? Of course."

"'Yes' is the answer to your question, and this has been going on for some time, even though the government would pooh-pooh this idea less they lose control. Each sighting has to be recorded, and seeing is believing."

"Enjoy the interest, for the interest keeps minds moving in that direction, for the pronouncement of the City of Light now hooked into The Light Center coming forth, will report many such informational appearances which makes itself more valuable day by day."

"Planet earth will see peace!" "Planet earth will know peace as it has never known before except before man entered the picture. All will be corrected and the war lords will war no more. This is a promise!" **So Light it be!**

Of UFOs and Human Fears

February 15, 2009

Question: "The City demonstration arrival in this country will look like a UFO has landed and fear would be automatic except for us Light Workers who look forward to space visitors. How is this to be taken care of with the United States government, as most sightings are kept secret except for several presidents who acknowledge they have physically seen one or more sightings and have told publicly of these sightings?"

ANSWER: "Recognize this country and the rest of the planet is basically fear based and that anything unusual would immediately trigger that fear of being attacked. The unknown can always hold a measurement of fear, and again it is survival at all costs. The pre-ground work is being studied and set into place. Pre-work has been set long since and as you read in the magazine this morning, the push is on to be what you are in truth."

"PURE LOVE and this is what is being remedied, and the message envisioning of the City is already activated."

"Several Presidents are already open to something new and UFOs seen periodically makes for more government secret interests to begin and adds to the previous sightings. The UFO community has long since been activated in promoting UFO activity in your world. This will not go unnoticed. First steps first."

GENII: "Will the City just magically appear with no advance notice or is there to be some pre-demonstration to sort of set the scene for this?"

ANSWER: "It is advised the Genii return to the City Embassy of Light Headquarters for this answer, as it is a bit complicated in your language vernacular and you, too, need to know the pre-steps of the demonstration to be witnessed. What can be reported at this inquiry is that all pre notifications will be in place. So line up your questions and return to the council. They will be prepared to take you forward and fear will not be looked at as a major problem. Your President Obama will be a major player in this scenario . . . so proceed."

GENII: "Anything else?"

ANSWER: "Remain in a stable condition for your job has just begun and has all the earmarks of this major event to elevate you in mind quickly. Permit any daily concerns to leave, as this takes precedence over any and all. Time, as has been said, is in short supply and your mental is needed to proceed as a high level ambassador of mental programming of this event. And as the Charles says 'all is well', and we agree." **So Light it be!**

Cities of Light – The Genii Connection Report

June 6, 2007

Q: "Please explain to me why so many people see so many different cities of light?"

A: "As The Genii has reported, the City of Light demonstrating in the Sedona area is the major first. Many have also seen what appears to be just that, cities of light that are all perfect, all heavenly, for if it were otherwise, like cities of darkness, it would not be reported in the same way."

"Visionaries from time immemorial have looked to a heavenly vision to sustain them, especially in times of pain. So then what is being seen and forecast as the immaculate heavenly adornment to come forth?"

"The Genii loves the castle of the Disney. Another sees streets of gold and jewels. You all seek the splendor of the visions as you walk the yellow brick road to the Oz of your delight, depending on the visions and the make-up of your mindset that bring forth the comfort in many ways."

"Then, included in this, comes The Genii with printed blueprints of a technical healing City of Light, not so much of a fantasy castle but one of solid advanced healing techniques of another kind. A City people can walk into and get healed from any source of pain through the medium of advanced lighting properties which she never knew about until the Rev. Dr. Bill Townsend brought through the designs during an altered awareness state of meditation (of which he was a master) that he, too, never knew of. This is called a clear transmission or trans-audio, with no human mental interference."

"What would people say if the City, dressed in the splendor of God, really looked totally like the fantasy of the mind? Maybe, 'Oh, this palace is beautiful and holy. Could this really be from God or another Disney attraction and how did it get here and where was it before?'"

"Dear ones, dreamers dream, paint pictures and bring forth desires one way or another. So let us take the dreamy design of fantasy and add solid advanced healing techniques plus places within the City structure where people can temporarily stay while others are being light attended in the light models, and even play a bit of golf in a nearby park."

"You say this sounds strange, playing golf in a holy materialization of a City of sacredness. We who dictate this recognize that human desire to have a place of comfort as well as healing, as comfort helps the healing, so why not include provisions for the comfort of those who enter into this domain of the Almighty?"

"Human people need to be able to accept what they are used to in a structure the minds can accept. Add the fantasy of storybook dwellings and the advanced (beyond your scope of healing at this point) and you have what is about to be demonstrated. The City of Light has it all; beauty, fantasy, space technology and a feeling one has indeed come home."

"All the cities talked about and seen have been brought into play to get humans ready to accept the big event, even back to the Bible, the Koran the ... the ... the ... and the list is endless, depending on the minds that create it in vision form."

"It will take just one City of Light to make all the dreaming visionaries say, 'Yes, this is what I saw when the plans The Genii is the gatekeeper for, are revealed.' All will mentally relate one way or another. It is all the same, just different minds in a dream process."

"Is the City of Light of first appearance the earth-shaking prophesy come true? We, the Intelligence that has followed this matter for centuries, declare here and now that what is to manifest is all one and the same."

"It is all the visions rolled into one, designed to attract everyone's attention from the human sleep state they have been in for even much length of your non-time span. The minds will then fill in the mental linking up of visions. But first there must be the grand opening for those minds to attach to in form."

"The City of Light that is to demonstrate may be slightly different in form, but one they can all relate to as their visions are validated. God has supplied and brought forth that which is the 'attention getter' to establish new methods of healing that all can and will be subject to."

"This is such a priceless gift from the universe that no one will care what was seen before, as it is the here and now that will make everyone a believer, believe you me!"

"Make way for the new, people, never before expressed in this way, for indeed the City of Light holds many rose gardens just for the pleasure of it."

"Release the old thoughts and move into "the new imagination" of possibilities never before heard of. You will be glad you did, and so will the God you worship!"

"We bid you the light of the eternal day in peace and love."

Blessings from The Genii

Seeing Cities of Light through Many Eyes

Question: "Why are different Cities of Light are seen by people?

"Each person is a mental artist with City designs given them that their systems can handle. In times of NDE or extreme circumstances or even in a quiet meditation state, Light in the form of Cities can be received and of course this is all good. The NDE experience with the lady and her favorite dog was a blessing to her in the reunion."

"Dreams of heaven on earth, are dreams of better times to come. These are all mental visions that not only impress, but can make believers out of non-believers, as most of this kind of imprint stays in the memory to be relived for its pleasantry for they are clearly magnificent."

"You on the other hand did not have the original vision the Dr. Bill, did as he was in a meditative place to be told what to put on paper as the basic design. You learned of it due to the sound conferences that you audio taped and asked questions that really had no connection with you, as you only took down what was being said. The visions were given to him and he in turn to you."

"Now however you have been trained as a so called 'sensitive visionary' and can readily see what is behind the dimensional veil of this City of Light prototype through your Inner City visits, thus expanding on the original which is more like a normal retreat or resort location with glorified internal structures that will lift the minds into paradise. Would God give Spirit any the less?"

"Were the visions really seen by others? Of course! Fantastic visions to delight the senses. How wonderful to have so many people being lifted through their own visions that somewhere in the ethers there are Cities of Light if only in a personal vision. Somewhere over the rainbow there is an Emerald City and they may be the first ones to enjoy the view for themselves."

"Praise God, Allah, and all the titles you put on the ONE for giving such a gift. Even if for just a few moments as they had made contact some place, somehow, somewhere in time.

So Light it be!"

Time Warp

Morning Message November 15, 2006

Q: "The e-mails now reporting the Mayan calendar is active for December 21, 2012 as a major event to take place. This prophecy has been noted for centuries, with the repeated references that Charles and I play a major part. What can be said of this and The City demonstration and our part in this? Advise please."

A: "What has been reported for centuries is a belief that has taken form after so many repeats of belief. The way of Light knows no limit and so as a certain date appears and re-appears the minds connected say, 'Yes, this is so!' When enough directives come into play from such writings, the world finds many ways to attune to the premise and as The Genii has said many times 'the mind can justify anything'".

"Now then, what validity has this announcement? Depending on the amount of belief and the ways of saying such, the interest builds to a peak, and the masses intertwined bring forth a mental equal to say, 'I knew it was so'".

"The Genii has been advised of a Healing City of Light that is to make a dramatic impact on the planet in which she, Charles, Starr-Light and others are tuned into this dramatic earth awareness event. As the minds validate the 2012 date and anticipate something spectacular to be attended to, the spiritual and physical continue to do just that, change, taking consciousness to a higher frequency peak."

"So then, what happens as the people attend their attention to the so called dates and then something spectacular demonstrates and catches them off guard as is said, 'like a thief in the night? The world of light workers say, 'halleluiah!' The planet change makes its mark, and darkness is no longer in charge through deluded minds holding the planet's progress with doubt and failure, and even the 2012 date is forgotten, for before their eyes it shines like something that cannot be denied . . . ever! Dates matter not . . . what does matter is the Holy Event itself!"

"Now then, why are you and the Charles and the Starr-Light and others, which are many, involved? Why not? Have you not, through the Dr. B, been given the actual plans of such an edifice? Have you not been told for years you are to carry this design in your heart and speak only when you are told to? Of course!"

"As the power of the light frequencies change your physical and mental knowing, its appearance will also take a quantum leap and the Charles, being assigned as the masculine part in all this, and the Genii, playing the feminine counterpart as has been said numerous times, you together bring to the world a new world as a connecting force of frequency power strong enough to demonstrate what has been so long in the quiet, yet progressing into the physical."

"Lay not aside these plans, for they will indeed shake up this planet as an earthquake awakens. You have both agreed in the unknowing senses that what you are about is valid and important and to pay strict attention, leaving no stone unturned, for value is to be found under each one, not darkness."

"Are your combined efforts to bring forth the City of Light? Does not the sun shine even when the clouds cover it?"

"Dear ones, indeed, one day the Genii and the Charles will say, 'Yes, it is done', and the Christ Consciousness is released like a Genie from a bottle with a knowing, introduced from within, that you both will know when it is to appear."

"Support each other, stay in the tune with the Word and all will be well with each one, for this is the message of the day.

So Light it be!"

Planet Peace Time Line

Morning Message January 1, 2008

Q: "As the New Year has arrived in a world of no time, and the City of Light moves closer to demonstration, what can be told of it and any part that I am to be supportive of?"

A: "The Genii remembers most of the City design and the layout described by Dr. B. This is just a beginning indicator of what is to come about (the first step, so to speak). There is much more attached now to the original, and you can find all the unprinted clues as you venture back into the inner visions given you."

"The time/date of the City appearance has always been 'under wraps' for the unknown is better kept that way for now. However, since the Genii has asked, it can be said that in the years coming forth and the changes now in process pulls the City energy also forward into being. It has been said over and over, 2012."

"This is incorrect in that by that time corrections in process now are seen to be completed and the manifestation has already been activated and recognized as such. That the masses from certain religions had declared, 'The second coming has arrived! The Messiah has come back, praise God!' For the Genii to enter the City for the healing data already given, these mental visions should continue on a regular basis, not only for information, but for imprinting it within you."

"Recognize your position here with the City of Light and accept as such. This is important so as you speak of this Holy event you can come from total knowingness and power."

"The City of Light, as you know, is total in its healing properties and facilities to accomplish the same on the earth ground in this dimension fed through alternative universes. All will work to bring forth what is unseen at the moment. One does not see a flower until it appears above ground. We have the same type of idea here. Then comes the AHHHH!"

"The Light Technicians have the mental ability to heal on the spot, so to speak, (remind you of a Master who walked your earth?). In the Light Pods in the City Modules they are able to help the patients in feeling comfortable enough to accept the healing lights of various kinds, and heal they do! "

"Remember people reject to various degrees what they do not understand, especially with the huge, massive demonstration never before ever see in history now standing in front of them not to be hidden. So before the City appears, mental changes must take place, and are, even as this is being recorded."

"The Genii is well aware of releasing, as she has been so called 'put through the ringer' lately, and keeping balanced through all the past fears, etcetera, coming topside to be released as the nothing that they are, has been a journey of courage. This is to be commended."

"This year will reveal the Power of the Jedi within you, as you were given a sample of recently, given at your favorite playground with the Charles who supported your strange behavior. This imprinting was deliberately given you so you could sense what it is to be in 'Total Power' and could pull it back in mind again when needed as old fears try to re-enter and no space is available. This is energy in action."

"So as you and the Charles again join forces to begin a new year of advancement, just remember to return to the City Envisions for more Light Imprinting and also when on the human plane, where you have just decreed that this 2008 will be a year of FUN, which everyone could use more of, all year long."

So Light it be.

A New World Now In Progress

January 2, 2001

"We shall begin again . . ."

"Humanity in its isolation upon this planet at this point, is not fit to interact with the Intelligence of older galaxies throughout the cosmos! We the intelligences are assisting to change this picture even as we speak in this moment."

"This information has been said before and it is being brought back into your minds due to the very slow process of your past teachings which for the most part are incorrect and keep you locked up in misinformation thus slowing your personal progress."

"You who are listening to this message have come a ways down the path (so to speak). You have been not only introduced to the sacred information hidden in the Four Keys but have also gone through the power of the lights in a process called 'linkage'".

"This as you know was not just a thing one would do for amusement but one of holy and sacred connection with God. You were chosen!"

"Why? Why would one be chosen? An ego aggrandizement perhaps? No! A way of saying I am more than someone else? No! A mark of achievement, Yes."

"You were chosen because you chose to be chosen and the Father/ Mother God said yes."

"So then, you have been given a gift is this not so? What have you done with that gift of advancement? Have you tucked it away with other precious items in your possession keeping it for some future time or have you taken this gift and used it wisely?"

"Have you refreshed your memory on the Keys as to their purpose? Have you understood their purpose? If not have you asked for help with an inner guide or outer guide?"

"Have you taken the time to give your personal guiding Intelligence a call asking questions? Have you received a reply? If you feel not, why not? Channeling is part of your gift given upon your 'linking' day."

"It is time dear ones, to take a good look at just what you have done with the keys of light so far. By this time, most of you should be able to Tone on the wind your praises to God. "

"You should be demonstrating before you even ask. You should be in such close contact with your guide and gatekeeper you all breathe at the same time for they are not separate from you."

"You should have pulled yourself up from being a low esteem victim of past events into the Greatness the Father/Mother Godhead knows you to be. . . that which you really are."

"You are seeking the 'real' you. Not the personality that hears this. You are multifaceted. God ! How many more ways can this be imprinted in your mind?"

"Can this God gift be taken away? Does God take away gifts not revered and tended?"

"God does not take away gifts the student quietly gives it back when not used as it was designed to be used. "

"What then is being said here? There is an old saying on your planet …'use it or lose it'".

"Now in the time of your new year so called, it is important that you take a good look at what has been given from the unseen, your reason for being on this planet at this time in your history has also been delivered, but has yet to come into view. This is where your devotion to God comes into play."

"You have been advised of the City of Light that has ascended on your planet. A healing place of such beauty and scientific advancement that it would take your breath up in awe to see it in all its splendor. It has within the grounds certain aspects that would help bring it into your seeing when you use what has been given to you."

"So then, you are all being admonished to separately daily, during you devotion to God work, to begin to bring that portion of the city into your mind for viewing and power. "

"You must have a sincere love to help bring this massive healing energy into the World of Illusion and requires your time and your tones daily thus you become an important part of the demonstration."

"So, this being said. We leave you to your decisions and bid you the LIGHT of the Eternal day in peace and in love."

So Light it Be……..

A Universal Cosmic Community

August 22, 2008

This morning while doing some paperwork I began to feel quite sleepy. I tried to ignore it but it persisted and then hearing to "go to the City" several times from within I finally gave up; I stopped my world and sat down to envision.

I was invited to go back to the gate complex, and did, as my usual guide/entity La-Luke took me by the left hand. He seemed excited plus in a hurry, so we ran through the gate and then the flowering park I had been to before.

LA-LUKE: "It has been some time since you have returned."

GENII: "What's up?"

LA-LUKE: "New life is being put into place."

We ran for some time until I could see in the distance something shinny black with a silver dome. Pushing aside low hanging tree branches, we came to an opening.

There was a huge, and I mean huge, space ship that was lowering a building into place that looked completed. It was like an elevator going down, lowering the building.

GENII: "Oh my God", was all I could mutter. "What is this?"

LA-LUKE: "This, Dear One, is why the City of Light does not need to be constructed on a site. This is done elsewhere and brought here ready for viewing."

GENII: "You mean all the buildings you have taken me to have been flown in? From where?"

LA-LUKE: "You would say outer space."

GENII: "Good Lord! Where in outer space?"

LA-LUKE: "Many planets and star clusters have wondrous healing methods of various kinds not seen or developed on your planet. I wanted you to see and know that the City has light instrumentation from many parts of the cosmos. You could call it a cosmos community of Star beings working together to bring harmony through light frequencies to heal this beautiful planet."

GENII: "Imagine that! I am in awe at what I am seeing and hearing. It kind of puts a piece of the City puzzle in place for me. Thanks!"

Due to the energy around this action we did not go any nearer, but much activity was certainty apparent. The entities around it were too far distant to make out any distinctive descriptions.

GENII: "What is this building used for that is now being set in place?"

LA-LUKE: "This building will be occupied by Light Technicians. Healing of the lower extremities like hips, legs, feet, et cetera, is the prime considerations that humans have, from broken bones to those who have perhaps lost a leg or two."

GENII: "I can hardly wait to ask this question: Can an amputated leg be replaced?"

LA-LUKE: "Yes, to a certain extent. The leg may be gone but the light imprint is still in place, and that is why people can still sense it is there once in a while. Or if desired, an advanced light body leg can be put in its place that is made of light. This is a longer story, but dramatic miracles, as you would call it, can take place here for those who want it."

GENII: "Surely someone in that condition would want an improvement?"

LA-LUKE: "Not necessarily. Some may be quite comfortable, as the tender care from loved ones affords them loving attachment to remain the same."

GENII: "Would you believe that!"

As I continued to watch the action for an unknown length of time, the building had settled down.

LA-LUKE: "So then moving entire buildings has been observed. Now departure time nears."

And almost immediately the spacecraft turned on and spun around, which sent frequency waves all the way to us who were just watching.

These crafts may be UFOs to many, but to me they are priceless vehicles that are here in service. And don't anyone ever try to convince me that they are here to conquer! P-L-E-A-S-E . . . to me they are welcome. And so desired ...very!

What a sight it was as it hovered, and then in a flash took off and was unseen. La-Luke took me back to the gate entrance bright eyed and in astonishment.

Imagine that!

So Light It Be.

More About a Universal Cosmic Community

August 23, 2008

GENII: "Tell me more please re: the space ships of light."

LA-LUKE: "The attributes of the space vehicles has much power, so much so that it can deposit a building on you planet dimension yet can fly from cosmic spaces light years away. How is this done, you might ask?"

GENII: "Yes, please."

LA-LUKE: "In other dimensions it is almost weightless."

GENII: "What?"

LA-LUKE: "In your world a big plane can carry many passengers and have the power to do so. The maintenance of the space ships has enormous value because it is able to transport a heavy object to its new location. This is why when you and the Dr. Bill thought that you were to build this city that you were told it was unnecessary.

"The cosmic community is also vast. The impression that some have that this is the one and only live-living-people planet in the universe is kindergarten thinking and we laugh as this is ludicrous!"

"Now than multitudes of star entities have united in the comforters of contribution of support in that recognizing the continuation of this beautiful planet vowed it should be helped in a different way so people could not only resonate to the higher creator but make it one that could never be ignored."

"So the City of Light comes into form to do just that, to be a manifestation in its scope never before experienced and one that could bring people into a healing of themselves that does not take centuries to find the answers of just how to do that."

"This City happening has been in prophecy in many cultures, in many ways, just not perhaps in this form. Small imprints have been seen here and there in the minds that are open to receive, and most were dismissed as a figment of an imagination. Now, however, comes the crème de la crème, many buildings of healing have been exposed to you, with many more to follow."

"Stay in the light, return and see advancement beyond your planet come into view. Then spread the word that God in its glory has brought forth the highest, dedicated to teach that God really exists for it will make believers believe you me, as you would say, and no one will ever go back to the old warn out ways of thinking how this all came about. The glow rays of prayers have brought forth the greatest show on earth that has ever happened."

"Yes, and all will bow down that such a creator exists. The Holy City of God then rests in the hands of the people. What will they do with it? Even that needs to be discussed. Time will tell...time will tell."

"So Dear One, go and seed the world with really new thought. Charles is your strong back up in support as well as Kathie and others to come on board, as well as a few million space friends who bring forth this magnificent manifestation called the City of Light!"

So Light It Be...Now!

The Feminine Place

September 3, 2008

Normally I have gone on these visits on my own. This is the first visit I have taken someone with me…….. Kathie Brodie.

As the inner vision began on this quiet morning in Sedona I see Kathie and me at the South Gate that I always pass thru. It is clear that my friend Kathie is with me on my right side. She looks astonished at this gate of entrance and beauty reaching five stories high encrusted with gems of very large size.

This visit is a kind of an experiment where someone enters with me and it seem to be working. I hope Kathie enjoys what she did and said, as I have no concept of what will take place until it does.

It was here we were met not by my usual guide but by a beautiful female entity wearing sheers of rainbow colors. She beckons us to follow her. I mentally asked the name of this guide and she says Tula.

As we entered, the park was still there. Kathie headed for the massage bench I had spoken of before, and the look on her smiling face said it all. Tula moved ahead and we followed thru the low hanging willow trees. Tula then made a quick right turn and we entered yet another path of exploration.

Now where, I wondered? Kathie was busy taking in all the sights with relaxed pleasure. Ahead was a group of see-through entities, all female, who smiled at these new visitors as we passed.

We climbed a small hill-like bump on the path to see another white building already in place. It had a two-story high horseshoe shaped glass (I guess) window and doors so you could see thru into the interior. Oh my, it was beautiful! Humm. Obviously God only knows beautiful, I thought, because everything just is!

We entered this massive gazebo type circular place with a ceiling that held birdcages and long lines of flowers. There were flowers everywhere. I could hear water tricking down over rocks, some seen, some not. The sounds of harp tones filled the air, and I figured we had just entered heaven somehow.

TULA: "This is a holy place of the feminine."

We both could feel that if not, we really needed a healing of some sort. Tula bid us to sit on this padded couch-like "seat", or whatever they call them. "This is called THE FEMININE PLACE!", Tula said.

Kathie asked: "What happens here?"

TULA: "The female of your species forgets her inner beauty, and for the most part has to take on the masculine to survive. Here she has a chance of healing and reigns in her goddess image she was born with in the first place, no matter what the world thinks of her and she has accepted as truth, and thus has to subject herself to the truth. Here she in re-imprinted to remember what she came into the world to be . . . feminine."

Kathie remarked that what she feels in this place was the totality, that everything, unlike her previous feeling, was changed. She thought it was great to feel so feminine and she felt balanced and it was strong within her.

Tula smiled, nodded, and said, "One has only to come in, relax, enjoy the viewing and accept all the working if this place to bring forth the feminine that you are and were encoded with when you arrived as female, and for the most part have set aside to care for your human world."

GENII: "This place puts you in sort of a meditative state and I feel different."

TULA: "How different?"

GENII: "Just like a new part of me has been added or something has cleared away." Kathie nodded. Genii said, "It is wonderful being a girl. Is this just because we are here?"

TULA; "Yes, this building is designed to heal from the inside out and to bring forth the original designed woman you are suppose to be, not as you do in your world in needing a make-over. You show that you feel."

KATHIE: "Will this knowing end when we leave?"

TULA: "No, this is why this is a healing place; that in which the self worth is brought forth and the old programming is expelled. No need to keep going in for more treatments. It is done here just by being inside. Of course this change over will need some new thinking as well, but why not feel beautiful all the time and not have to search for it on occasion?"

GENII: "Do the males have a place too?"

TULA: "Oh yes, the Masculine Place! The gender of the male is different so the frequencies inside are different to draw to itself what the masculine was born to be. Men have desires not spoken of to the female and need also to remember the sacred part of them, so the Masculine Place takes care of that on all levels."

"So then this is the discovery of the Feminine place. Remember it when you are back in your world, and take these frequencies enjoyed here, the sights and the sounds, with you."

Tula got up as harp music of some kind that seemed to verify what we were sensing began to play and she and led us back to the glass entrance. We almost floated, but since we were not used to floating yet, we walked.

It is hard to explain the changes we felt we had dropped off like an outer garment revealing the god light we had brought forth. Kathie just glowed, as I have never seen her before.

A last glance around was an invitation to return again, for our true feminine was in place. The gardens, the birds and flowers on long vines did leave an impression, as did the water sounds.

Wow... Women will sure want to experience THE FEMININE PLACE.

Imagine That!

The Feminine Rejuvenation Temple

August 13, 2009

"Be Ye Renewed By the Renewing Of Your Mind"

The way was made clear to reenter the City of Light by watching whatever appeared on my screen of space. The 4 Keys to Light classes I share with others have taught me well. This is only the second time I have taken someone with me. I looked to enjoy what she and I would see, as no previous indication was apparent.

Arriving at the usual Gate of Receiving, I meet my guide, La-Luke, my guest Amayra and a Guide of hers. We enter the Park of Relaxation where she seems to be beaming, as she rested on a massaging bench, which began to massage her back. She snuggled into it but not for long as we moved through the massive willow trees, moving their branches aside like curtains ready to see the show. We traveled onto a path unknown to me.

"Where are we going?" I asked my Guide.

LA-LUKE: "Ah, yet another Building of Receiving," he replied. We seemed to walk quite a ways past previously-seen buildings, which were all in white with gold trims. "Exquisite!" I remarked silently to myself.

My guest tried to take in everything she could as we suddenly turned to the right and to a beautiful building more like a temple, which I had not seen before but I recognized, like all the rest, this was a healing facility of some sort.

GENII: "What is this place?"

He just smiled and bid us enter what looked like one of those doors that one can revolve in like in hotels here. Inside this building we see what is called a Transforming Welcome Station. Transforming what? Oh, well, we felt it was great just being in the City.

The look on Amayra's face said she concurred. The lobby, like many others, had a bubbling fountain off to one side that made a tinkling sound as the droplets hit the bottom.

Suddenly a female who appeared kind of transparent (which I call a see-through) came into view and requested the male guides stay put and requested that we women follow her down a very high-ceilinged corridor. On the walls of the corridor and up to the ceiling there were vines of some sort where pink and white tiny flowers bloomed and they had a sweet scent that was delicious.

Our corridor trip was a short one, as yet another circular room with yet another waterfall and strange music coming from somewhere unknown came into view. At this point several transparent ladies appeared in flowing pastel-colored gowns. They beckoned us to follow as they laughed. Their laughter in itself is healing.

We are now at another room with a very large overhead screen and are invited to lie on the lounges provided and requested to just rest, so we do. As we do, the screen above gave us the instructions in English of what was to come next.

We were to watch our earlier lives come forth in picture form, and when we saw a time we thought of ourselves as beautiful, young, vibrant, healthy and happy, to stop at that point and keep this mental image firmly in place. We went through being born into this life, the teen years, young adults, et cetera. The interesting part also was that even though there was only one large screen, we only saw our own life. Cosmic stuff to be sure. Why not?

I picked the time I was satisfied with what I saw and I can only suspect she did too. We were then to mentally imprint that sight we liked as an up-to-date memory clip that would sustain no matter what age we became, even 209. Fascinating! Two female entities came over and though no audible words were heard, one told us that we would always look like that, first to ourselves, and then to others. This was a MIND MAKE-OVER. Imagine that!

A bevy of angel-type giggly female entities gathered around as we lifted off the lounges. We human females looked at each other and joined in with the attendees. Indeed, years had fallen so as to be nonexistent. So much for all the cosmetic and surgery used now these days to do what we can see happened here. Let's hear it for this type of makeover. Whoopee!

We left the building feeling great with no memory of aging. It was all a mental makeover. We headed back to our male guides who grinned, as they knew what was going to take place with becoming the new us. We came in as one person and got the thrill of any lifetime.

The women will get in line for this kind of delightful experience. The new us left the building escorted back through the park and to the Gate of Entrance with our memory healed, to only be the person we had chosen to look like and be. Thanks God!

Back in Sedona I could see many ready to get a memory makeover. This has been a fun trip that indeed would change our lives forever. So that is the City of Light Rejuvenation Temple. It will indeed be a favorite place for women, in particular, to visit. Imagine that!

So Light It Be.

Inner Workings Beneath The City Of Light!

October 10, 2008

Reentering the City can take many levels of consciousness. When you have achieved a certain level of consciousness, the passage will be accomplished. This time the passage or visit was designed to take us beneath the City. It is a city within a city.

Massive in its undertaking, it is awesome beyond awesome is the closest I can come to expressing. The mechanics of running such an overhead vehicle, which the power of God itself envisioned, must be something to behold.

Computer types of different kind and most not ever seen before process the above, with huge wall-size screens on which visions of the City above are captured. Many entities are active and actually possess the computer light information themselves, like walking computers, of each building above. Now I am saying these are "computers", as this is my current knowledge of them, but they are much more complicated than that.

This underworld is an electromagnetic field all of its own, and one would think with all this machinery it would be quite noisy but it is totally silent, putting me almost into a meditative state. It is not dark inside, either, but daylight bright. The computers seem to be attached to whatever building of healing or light standards above. My vision is limited in expressing the massive effect all this has on me, a world unknown yet producing a world above for our visions and healings to be applied.

Going to the moon was child's play compared to what makes this City of Light light up. I am assuming that what makes this City function is in place before it appears, yet I am informed not so. All is connected.

Space Scientific Advancement

October 12, 2008

GENII: "Embellish please. What make the City of Light light?"

ATHERIAN: "Precisely that, electrical frequencies patterned throughout the inner workings of the electromagnetic field on which the city is dependant. This is no ordinary field, as you might surmise."

"This City information is so far advanced that we who speak on this have a difficult time of explanation in your language, which is always a problem, for the oratory access is unavailable in our sensing. You people need a new way of working with the intelligence of guide speakers who bring forth this information. You are so far behind that new schooling should be put into action and thus all advanced information is understood immediately."

"Recognize this is a massive undertaking, scientific beyond scientific in your eyes. It was once said to the Genii that you have no idea of what it takes to bring in to your dimension this big a process, not at all, the likes of which have never been seen before, nor duplicated since. That in itself, of course, is a mystery."

"You have seen the huge computer types?"

GENII: "Yes"

ATHERIAN: "Then replicate that by thousands, all tuned into the one source of creation."

GENII: "Directly tuned in?"

ATHERIAN: "Yes, this master creation is seen as the City which was developed in another dimension so advanced that just the thought of it makes it feel almost non- existent in a reality that is much different than yours, yet explosively predominate, on certain levels. The processing of the City entrance into your world is like the Immaculate Conception, to say the least. Ancient teachings in your world say anything is possible for those who believe."

"As the belief systems change, and change they must, swinging away from the non-belief to the now-belief, the City comes faster into view. The earth minds vacillate continually, as you know. One second is 'this', and then 'that'. And this produces instability for perhaps a few seconds or longer, depending on the topic of conversation you have within the confines of your brain; a changing of the guard, so to speak, a change-over from old, slow thinking to a speeding up."

"At this point you have many accredited teachers who share information to further your lives, and rightly so; however, recognize that behind their word they, too, need what is being said to you. They are teaching themselves constantly in learning."

"So, then, the demonstration of the City is run by electrical beings."

GENII: "Electrical beings?"

ATHERIAN: "Precisely so. You are an electrical being, are you not, different from those who are programmed to work the computer types in a high state of advanced awareness?"

GENII: "Like what is being told to me, that I should begin teaching in the Light Center through the Advanced Achievement Academy?"

ATHERIAN: "Quite so. It is a better start than what is being produced."

GENII: "Are these electric beings robots?"

ATHERIAN: "Not as you know think of them currently. Again, your language has difficulties. We are not avoiding the answer however we invite you to just think of the energy coming through the High and Gate Towers. These and many factors are connected to produce the underside and the compact elevation of the overhead intricacies you are being advised of. Eons of city programming keeps the City safe under any circumstances, as it freely gives of itself in the advanced healing ways now being addressed."

"This is just a brief indication of what your extreme scientists will find fascinating to see and learn. You have said that God has something wonderful coming into view, and so it is ... indeed!"

"So for this brief moment in time this short glimpse given you expands your awareness just a bit. Remain in your wonder of it all, for more inner visits will astonish you and you will be encouraged to share the information. Your guide will meet you at the gate and you can proceed to be yet more enlightened with what is coming about, and soon."

So Light It Be!

The Be-ing Building

January 11, 2009

As before, once again I find myself at the Gate, but I know not which one. It seems to be the only one in sight, anyway. As I enter the scene, crowds of smiling people are also entering. This new site challenges any belief system that something like this could really take place right before their eyes. I enter with the rest of the crowd

The park is filled with happy faces in awe of this exposure. This is obviously not a private vision tour today for me, at least at this moment. People move in streams going here and there to explore this not-man-made extravaganza. I just mill around watching what is taking place, mostly in disbelief.

As I follow a path veering off to the left, there is seen yet another building in the distance. At this point I continue to follow. No guide yet is seen. Many people have entered the grounds but no one is close to me as I am a distance ahead. The building is a distance from the Gate. I approach this building.

Comment: These building all seem to be white and gold so far.

It was then that my guide La-Luke appeared. He led me inside. Melodious sounds of an unknown origin spring out from unknown locations. The entryway had exploded into a sound chamber of sensing that hit my heart and emotions, so much so I was in bliss.

GENII: "What is this place?" I asked my guide.

"How do you feel?" he replied.

"I just do not have words to describe it. I am in such a state of 'nothing matters, this is all there is'. Have I come to heaven?"

He laughed. "Well, not quite. You are still alive. This is a healing sound building. You know when you feel a time out is needed, or as you say, stop the world I want to get off? Well, this is that place where the outside world stops and you are just, as you say, be-ing." "You might call it the Be-ing Building. This is more of a pass-through place that for a short period of time you have all the outer ingredients to entice you to just BE."

"With nothing to prepare beforehand, we just walk in and you get the feeling of be-ing. . . gentle, loving and restful, which tunes up the electrical system so much that you can face the outside world more easily just by having felt what it is like to just BE. As you are human beings, you need to know what it is to just BE.
So you entice that feeling when the outside world gets a bit heavier. How do you feel now?"

GENII: "I feel wonderful, balanced and relaxed."

LA-LUKE: "Good. Then we have come to the end of this visit. Mission accomplished. Take this be-ing feeling back into your world and thus imprint others who enter your electrical space for a moment."

We walked out and back through the crowds of people, aah-ing and ooh-ing to the Gate of Light. I waved thanks to my guide, upon which I quickly found myself back home in Sedona feeling pretty good!

Thanks, God, for the visit to the Be-ing Building. It was great.

So Light It Be.

The City of Light Appears, Now What?

It was just to be a so-called normal day in the lives of people on this planet. It was planned through their mental equation of what they were planning to do that day . . . a normal day indeed . . . but the God Spirit had other plans.

It had long been said by many prophets on the earth that one day all would change for the better. Prayers for peace on earth and good will to men and women had long since sailed into the universe to be picked up by the highest deity of all.

But today, unknown to almost everyone, this was to be totally different from any other day ever remembered in the history of this planet. This was to be the City of Light's introduction to the world.

Was it a dream, an outward/inward vision presenting itself? Sure we had seen the Virgin Mary on various tree trunks, etc., but this sight was beyond all that. Surely people thought that they were losing their minds because when they went to sleep there was nothing there, and now . . .

Call the Dalai Lama, call the Pope, call somebody, anybody, to tell him or her what was taking place. Validation of sanity was needed here and now!

Quickly, upon noticing something had been added since the night before, the media picked up this unusual edifice now shining brightly, as if no sun was needed that day, and indeed it wasn't.

The government quickly sent out the Air Force jets to see what had taken place. Protection at all costs was in strict force, but due to the light being emitted from this demonstration, they had a difficult time seeing what exactly it was that had caused so much excitement and even concern.

There were suddenly television stations recruiting reporters in mass to be the first ones on the "light spot" to cover the event. The current celebrities in the headlines were banished and forgotten, for something major had taken place… imagine that!

What was this place of light that, because of its brightness, could not be seen totally at first? Was this conquest from outer space? Extraterrestrials coming to get us? And what would they conquer . . . wars and fighting and egos gone wild?

Who in outer space wants that? We have been praying for eons of time for peace. Maybe we have embodied too many movies of violence coming from others not of our kind. They are probably only wanting to be of service, and not even thinking of taking over . . . please.

Maybe this place of glowing light was something that God /Spirit declared to come forth to heal this planet so that it could, for all intents and purposes, not be an outcast from the rest of the planets due to our low consciousness and fear of attack.

Just maybe, now the consciousness was being raised to the point that we could use some extra help, and it was definitely being supplied as an eye opener. This was something so big that people could begin to see this holy demonstration, as it was standing right before their eyes.   Could this be a wake-up call?

Upon seeing this magnificent manifestation, many fell to their knees in Holy Communion with the Source of their higher guidance systems, Buddha, Christ, and many other Masters who seem to have a hot line to the boss (so to speak), and many of those who seem to check in during meditation, as inner voices teach.

Many people went into delight and joy mixed with love, for it made a great empowering concoction. They knew that their prayers had been answered, in maybe a different way, but an answer they felt they had.

Many others, on the other hand, went into survival fear due to their previous mental program, for they had sinned or something, all of which is detrimental, of course, rather than a delightful experience.

As long as the Christ was still coming (as in the second coming) they could still keep on sinning (meaning missing the mark) but maybe it was the energy of all the Masters, Saints, Angels and Guides who embodied Love manifested . . . maybe?

Maybe this City of Light just dropped out of the sky to get our attention as a healing place to begin heaven on earth. Maybe it was a gift that the God Spirit sent us to get healed from the mental to the physical to the emotions and all the rest. Maybe it was a validation that somewhere in the unseen it was declared that we needed an injection of love and light so strong that we had to have and see something so dramatic that it could not be denied.

Maybe this is the biggest blessing this entire world has ever experienced. The City of Light just appeared with no previous fanfare. It just appeared! Maybe from this experience we could learn more about the universe, that in its contents we could discover much more and we could use it to better our lives in more delightfully different ways than before . . . maybe!

The time had come for peace on earth. They were given a new way of looking at each other from the eyes of love, not of hate and vengeance and all the other horror stories flashing across our screens to promote more of the same negative thinking.

The time had come, for this unexpected Sight of Sights had brought with it in a split second a vision so strong that anything outside of love and truth was banished, and the consciousness was raised quickly. People felt that finally their prayers were answered, and guess what? They didn't have to lift a finger to bring it forth, only accept it in their mind, and they did, one by one and millions by millions.

Yes it was expected to be a normal day, sunrise to sunset, but in between this space of time something unusual took place and nothing would ever be the same again . . . ever. The City of Light became manifest on Earth!

Praise God! In love and expectancy.

Introduction to the City's Embassy of Peace Headquarters

Within the confines of the City of Light there is a spectacular building known as the Embassy of Peace Headquarters. It is dressed in white with gold exteriors that amplify the opulence of the City itself. Inside and outside, this building is surrounded by fragrant flowers of all kinds producing gardens of beauty that touch the senses full force. Breathtaking? Yes! Dramatic? Yes! Informative? Absolutely!

This is where I was invited to come and ask any questions of highly evolved entities who sat in readiness to deliver answers regarding the City, and even the universe if I so chose. How great is this?

To get there I was to meet with my Guide at one of the now familiar five-story high Gates leading into the City itself. To ride to this building we were carried on a wheel-less, driverless trolley-type vehicle. On my first visit inside we were met by several unidentified leaders of some sort who either sat or stood (to indicate respect) behind a horseshoe-type advanced apparatus, perhaps what we would call a table, but it was much more.

As we entered, I was led to a throne-like chair which I could only guess was for dignitaries. It was very plush and comfortable. "Yummy", was my silent inner response. What was behind them is what made this place awesome, for it was like a hollowed out amphitheater of hundreds of entities faintly seen but present nevertheless, like a cosmic community. Awesome!

So, then, the scene being set, I invite you to journey with me to listen in on the conversations that took place between those in command and the Earthling, me, collected throughout many continuing visits I have complied them here for your pleasure.

WELCOME TO THE

EMBASSY OF PEACE HEADQUARTERS

IN THE CITY OF LIGHT!

So Light it Be!

Genii's Visits to the Embassy of Peace Headquarters

The Invitation January 24, 2009

GENII: "In the sensing of yesterday's message that I am to speak to world leaders on the City, and now the Embassy of Peace, what would I say?"

ANSWER: "To re-enter the City and sit in Council with the Entities of Light would be advised. The major interests will become apparent, as the information given is subject to the questions to be asked."

GENII: "Who would be in this Council of Entities?"

ANSWER: "Those who could answer your questions."

GENII: "What if I don't know what questions to ask?"

ANSWER: "You will. The energy flowing like the intense feeling of yesterday will set the course."

GENII: "What am I to do to ready myself for such a vision meeting?"

ANSWER: "As usual."

GENII: "What does the Embassy of Peace, which seems to include the whole of the planet, intend to achieve?"

ANSWER: "Again, this session would bring to the forefront what is intended to be accomplished here."

GENII: "Are there more Embassies of Peace imprinted in the Cities' blueprints elsewhere on this planet?"

ANSWER: "One could say, as a starter, in the minds of those who cry for peace on earth."

"This is not a new concept. This peace idea has been in evidence for centuries as even a master walked the planet, and you know the story of what happened to him."

"Ignorance, darkness of the truth has gleamed many a war, be it on a battlefield of many or between two or more people who disagree on any particular subject. When anger flows, the energy rises to attack. When love flows, energy rises to heal."

"The Jedi motto decrees that never in attack, only in defense, and even if love were the defense, like the sword, the light would banish the darkness, for darkness cannot hold the energy when light is applied. The Force spoken of is love, not to be used in anger, and again, all is mental."

"The Embassy of Light regulates peace and healing as its objective, which will be and will be major in its refinement now in process. The more love given out, the faster the cleansing. As has been said, this planet is far too valuable to have its treasures destroyed. Those who do the dark work will have no recourse but to cease the destruction of the innocent people, animals and nature. Thus, the major decree has been given you."

"Are you destined to speak to world leaders in and out of authority? Yes."

GENII: "But I am basically unknown."

ANSWER: "You have been chosen. That is what you need to be aware of at this moment. We recognize being famous for any reason is not where you are coming from; however, this will take place anyway. You have an inner heart that loves, even as many noted masters have been so designed, with no other dream but to serve your God in unusual ways. And serve you do, so this is just one more way."

"A big one, to be sure, but massively important as you became very aware of yesterday. Will you be known? My, yes. You are being prepared even as we confer at this moment. Have you not said that this is your destiny?"

"At this point guidance has been given and your attendance in this court of the Embassy of Peace opens its doors for consultation with the highly respected Mind Masters who guide the makings of decisions, thus bringing forth what has been put on your plate of dreams for some space time now."

"Think on these things and we shall confer as you come to a meeting of Mind Masters, for indeed this is now possible. We await your entrance."

So Light it be

P.S. GENII: "Anything else to be addressed?"

ANSWER: "The message has been given for the moment. Stay tuned in, as more will be revealed in a split second. All is on course, of course."

Of War and Peace

Embassy of Peace Headquarters, January 22, 2009

Arriving at the City Gate, no one was seen. In fact, dark skies were apparent. The City was lit up like New Year's Eve. All my previous visits were in daylight. This was the first at night, and what an awesome light sight it is.

To see this location from space must be quite a sight to behold, as it made daylight seem obsolete in this City of Light. So once again I get to enter and learn more. Quickly, as I glance around, my guide La-Luke appears, and taking my hand, we enter into this vastness of this healing facility.

"Where to now?" I wondered. As quickly as I thought this, a moving trolley came up. If there was a driver there, one was not seen. We got on board and it began its journey, riding through spacious gardens and parks. There was just a glimpse here and there of buildings and we just rode for a bit. I was puzzled because this vehicle seemed to skim over the ground where no wheels or tracks were observed. There was just a free flow.

After stopping in front of another building dressed in white light, we entered. Inside were absolutely beautiful gardens with even a waterfall to enjoy, amidst this type of foliage.

"Where are we?" I asked, ready for anything to be reported.

LA-LUKE: "This is a building of human atrocities."

GENII: "What is that?" I wondered.

LA-LUKE answered, "That means peace is to be brought forth. The wars of mankind have long since been active. Here the ways of such are abolished in the minds and instead is embedded that no such thought is possible."

"Those who have been in war-like mindsets no longer will feel the anger and fear that brought it on in the first place. Man against man, brother against brother, no more! No more! The upper levels of this building are the remedy places where the energy fields of such thoughts are abolished, whether people are in here or not."

"It is a center location in the City to send forth such a magnetic field that eliminates any indication of war-like atrocities. This no longer will be tolerated. Nation against nation is abolished. Armies of protection are no longer needed, as peace is the only protection desired."

GENII: "You mean peace on earth can be obtained from this place? How is that achieved?"

We entered the building as before, finding ourselves again in front of the counselors, peace entities, where my question was answered.

OOO-LON: "By changing the frequencies from war-like intrusions to peace and love, which of course in your world has not been known to any major extent. The human cry of 'peace on earth' has sounded its tone throughout history. From this place, like other cities in the blueprint, this loving existence fulfills that prophecy through leveling of love instead of hatred and war."

"Anyone who enters here is cleansed of all that from the DNA mental equivalent to only know peace and love. They then, of course, take that into the world. As time enters, countries will only know and experience loving gratitude to be what they are in truth and see all others the same way, as one family unites with others as one."

GENII: "That is wonderful."

OOO-LON: "Anger and hatred are abolished totally, for each now is in the totality of peace within themselves. Children will learn of love, instead of the opposite. Sharing is fun instead of competition. Even in the competition, it is for the fun of the game and everyone wins."

"Recognizing this is a vast way of looking at a new beginning; nevertheless it is possible. So then, how feel you in this place?"

GENII: "Calm, centered and appreciative and filled up with love, yet amazingly my emotions are like this is normal."

OOO-LON: "Good, then. We have completed the vision trip for this time."

We exited this beautiful garden-type place where peace does reign supreme. We climb back on the wheel-less trolley and head for the gate. I wondered what the electric bill would be for the City of Light, but then it doesn't matter, for God has it well in hand, and a peaceful hand at that.

I say thanks to my Guide, he disappears and I am back in my warm cozy bed, a bit better off from having this strange experience of what is to come about.

Thanks, God. This is really a mind stretcher to be sure!

So Light It Be.

Additional Connection from La-Luke

EMBASSY OF PEACE HEADQUARTERS, January 23, 2009

OOO-LON: "This previous information just gives a hint of what it is about. It would be like connecting heaven and earth into one where, warring factors cannot co-exist with love being the linking force. When people are linked in light they have no conflict, for within themselves this is not tolerated or experienced. Love makes light apparent and as Atherian Light guide of the Genii has said 'WARS WILL END!'"

"You have the White House, we have the Embassy of Peace on the holy ground of the City of Light. As changes now in process with the appointed leader who basically is a peacemaker, this will eventually lead to the Embassy of Peace connection."

"There is much more to be said as this only gives a hint of the power and strength connected. Such changes that you have never seen before or imagined are in process and this is only the tip of the iceberg, so to speak in your vernacular."

"What you all are dealing with here is the makeup of the new world being prepared for you all to awaken to. Listen o Israel, for this is the monument in evolution where the power of God light stirs up the masses to accept God's will for indeed this is the appointed time of receiving long since spoken of in time related messages."

"God will bless and be blessed, for Light now removes all darkness to show the folly and ignorance contained within its borders of stress. Time is short."

"So the Embassy of Peace Headquarters now revealed to the Genii, stands within the City of Light as a beacon to all who would accept this as an omen of what is to come about and . . . come about it will! Make no mistake about that! Peace on earth? Oh my yes. . . beyond and faster than a speeding bullet can hit its target."

"So then continue to be open...report this and the previous visit to the Embassy for more will be added as you are walked forward in vision and the knowing that what you are about has no opposite and with this we leave you to your day that now flows into place."

So Light It Be!

GENII P.S. I just know that I am being set up to talk with world leaders on this topic. There is no ego attached; better to be on my knees in honor as the power coming through right now is awesome. Imagine that!

The Council of Master Minds Meeting 1

EMBASSY OF PEACE HEADQUARTERS January 27, 2009

Entering into a calm meditative state, I suddenly got the vision of being back into the gardenlike foyer of the building I had previously been in before with my guide, although he was not seen now. Appearing from an opening at the end of a corridor came an entity smiling and bowing. He beckoned me to follow him and clearly this was a sensing that I had arrived at my destination which I knew somehow was the Chambers of Masters.

As we went through the opening entrance, the vision was not a room as we know a room with walls, but something very different. Let's see how do I explain the unexplainable?

No walls and feeling of vastness as the air was filled with moving pictures floating gently and silently around and overhead. Kinda like being in the universe mentally. A kaleidoscope of pictured thoughts curling around! Who's thought? Why pictures? What is going on?

Had I stepped into the universal 'now' moment? It felt very peaceful and a feeling of love filled my heart. None of this would make much sense in my human thinking. But hey... if I was going crazy, it sure felt pretty good. Interestingly though, I am very clear headed and strong ... actually more than normal.

At ground level was seen a circular long table with one opening like a horseshoe. In that space was a throne-like chair in gold with pillows of blue/ purple colors. As I looked at the table, entities began to appear. Settling in, they took on the human exterior of male, female while love, strength and gentleness appeared from them, but with much power also. A light above each head cascaded down and around encasing them in its frequency.

I wonder if these are some of the Golden Illumined ones of the Court of the high tribunal I know about. I felt that this meeting was just to acclimatize me into this new way of accepting what was to come about. And that I was an honored guest sitting in this Throne of Excellence, as I was inwardly told it was, and believe you me, with what I was experiencing, it needed to be absorbed a bit to be understood.

It was a meeting of high level minds to be sure. The questions of Who? What? Where? and Why? were still to be introduced into verbal communication. Could my mind understand this enough to continue? Continue? Excuse me look how far you have come Genii...of course...I just needed a moment or two to absorb the ecstasy of it all. Was time a factor here?

Then an entity of light, male in design, which I felt was to give me some mental balance of identification stood up and smiled, giving me a hand signal of welcome.. Wow! Talk about being in a strange land. He opened his mouth to speak but no sound arrived to my ears. Then another entity tapped him on the arm and this person adjusted a ring on a finger and sound was heard like tuning up the volume on a radio.

With this I heard "Welcome to the City Council. We are the Ambassadors of Mental Light, the Mind Masters or the Master Minds of this City of Healing, that God has entrusted to bring forth what you have been part of before this life incarnation of space time."

"Since this is strange and must be absorbed, we invite you to do that, and come back as you need to, and we will once again enter into the conversational informational area where you will be comfortable and can understand clearly."

By this time I was getting very light headed so that felt right. With this he sat down but his light body aura stayed in form a bit higher, then slowly lowered surrounding him.

I thanked them and indeed I needed to adjust my thinking. Then this scene ended and I seemed to float back into my home and bed where most of my morning mediation takes place...I really was 'spacey' and felt to go outside for some fresh air . . . and I needed to do human things like take the trash out. Boy, that ought to do it!

Ok God. I will be back . . . This was really fun . . .

Thanks, Genii.

Conversation with A Commander of Space Light

EMBASSY VISIT February 2, 2009

Q: "Is it appropriate this morning to reenter the Embassy of Peace?"

A: "In the prospect of reentering the Embassy, 'Just do it...'"

As I envision myself again into this strange place, one would think I would be getting used to this. However, each visit is a phenomenon in itself. What was seen before was not even a room, as we know a room to be, but an empty space with pictures floating in the air; beautiful to be sure, strange also. This time there were no pictures floating anywhere. It was open at the top and the evening sky held it all together as stars peeked in to say whatever stars would say if they would say anything. Okay, moving on . . .

Again around this horseshoe-shaped table were faint entities, obviously leaders of some sort. Then one stood up and I could see him pretty clearly. He wore a white robe, gold belted. He was clean-shaven and appeared human-like, and most of the others did too. This could be to allow me to adjust to new energies, since I think they are from somewhere other than here.

"I am OOO-LON, Commander of the Space Light of your planet and keeper of information for distribution." His voice was stern. This, obviously, was a no nonsense guy, which was okay with me as I am the new kid on the block and am here to learn.

"I am not of your world but I am able to speak your language. As an earthling you have been summoned here, since you are a designated spokesperson for your planet and this healing edifice, so named the City of Light. Are you in agreement?"

Genii: "What does that mean, Commander of the Space Light?"

OOO-LON: "As said, the ways of your world have had many incarnations of Light in the time past and now it is different as we are Light within Light and our frequencies blend as one to supersede any areas that need being revised, and many do."

Genii: "Excuse me, as I am trying to understand beyond my current understanding as this is like a space video. I do sense much love with you all and I am trying to make sure I am not just dreaming this up."

OOO-LON: "Indeed you are not, for that would not be allowed and would do nothing to perpetuate the process. Space teachers we are, and the galaxies will benefit greatly from our contact. If agreed, we shall proceed."

I nodded my head yes and he said, "Good then, we shall proceed." The other entities smiled and I began to lighten up and smiled back in gratitude of what is being presented.

OOO-LON continued: "As an Assembly of Light Contactors, we have brought you here as an assigned Ambassador of Planetary Happenings that are taking place as light intensive embraces this planet into itself. We recognize this is all unusual for you; however, you will adjust quickly."

Genii: "I am open to that and the fascination of what I can be a part of in helping this planet in its own growth and the purpose of this City and its healing powers. How can I be of help? I am only one and many people have had far more spirit trainings than I have."

OOO-LON: "You think simply, almost child-like and not in an overload of mechanical pre-programming. This makes it easier for you to digest what you and we are about. What is being decreed on your planet for mandatory intervention of assistance of releasing the make-up of those who consistently stay in keeping the old and thus the turbulence continues, when we bring the way of peaceful intervention. "

"What has been obtained by aggression is to be ended. To assist in treating, more energy is bombarding this planet to raise the consciousness of those who have long since been in this state looking for answers that take too long to find. Many organizations work to achieve peace."

"Peace at all costs is in process and will continue, as it affects everyone. But even now, what has been currently imprinted is beginning to crack open what has been closed even as we speak. Your process is just that, in process. Be not concerned. We have chosen the right humanoid long before you entered this lifetime. Many Lightworkers all over this planet are in agreement, and that in itself is lifting the energy."

Genii: "And what is it that this Council does?"

OOO-LON: "This is why you have been invited to come and sit with us who are not of your planet, but part of a universal community sent to advise, guide into what is well taking place. This City is to be announced just by being revealed to the masses. That in itself will change the way people will look at this home base and themselves, as it will seem like a domino effect."

"This Peace Council recognizes that it has much work to do and in relatively a short time, but just one link like yourself connecting with another and then they in turn link others has much power attached. Peace will indeed be secured. There are, as you know, many organizations and corporations that, when they get past the greed of survival, will make an advanced leap of support and the frequencies will move much faster."

"The planetary progress of earth-grown produce must be advanced to survive. The green house effect must be looked at as a top priority, for those in this arena recognize this. Now the earth interior meets the sky exterior and you are sandwiched in the middle. This will continue for a while yet, but be aware that what is in change now will change the outer picture drastically, and this is all for the good and healing here."

"Many will leave, due to the intensity of the frequencies being felt. On the other hand, many will rejoice that such a happening is in process, which is not stoppable. We have been brought here to advise, guide and change the overall picture to be what is livable within the confines of your energy fields and the universe as well."

"So then this is just an indication of ourselves. In speaking of this to others, request questions and we will endeavor to answer them. Through love, God sent us, as this universal community seated here is just a fraction of what help is available."

"Peace at all costs. The cost is but to activate the intelligence within each one to extend a healing hand where you can. Key people could be set in certain positions like north, south, east and west, where they are familiar with what is taking place, and hold the energy there."

"So then this is just the beginning. Think on these things and we shall endeavor to precipitate something at our next meeting, and with that we bid you a 'God' day in every way."

He bowed, as did the rest, and I nodded in agreement. And with that, the vision ended and I found myself back in Sedona watching the sun awaken the red rocks on a Monday morning.

So Light It Be!

The Cosmic Raising of Consciousness

CITY OF LIGHT EMBASSY OF PEACE REVISITED, February 7, 2009

Re-entering while in a meditative state, the scene once again is at the Gate but this time several small children greeted me with smiles and led me thru the Park of Relaxation to where my friendly city guide, La-Luke, took over and the kids just disappeared. My guess was they headed for the playing field where a cloud of white mist can be grabbed as a snowball and tossed.

GENII: "Who are these children?" I asked

LA-LUKE: "They are young entities of parent entities who use this place as a playing ground just for the fun of it. Come, we venture to the Embassy as light attends those who await us."

With this, time seemed to move ahead very quickly and I found us in the place where see-thru entities as I call them stood around the horseshoe table in acknowledgement that we were present.

OOO-LON: "We welcome you back to this Council of Peace and Keepers of Advancement."

GENII: "What am I to know?"

OOO-LON: "The world of your economy is in a cleansing mode and upon the finish will be stronger than ever before, for people are now in mixed energies finding new ways to do old things. Those who seek employment will find new ways to incorporate old values and invent new ones. The current so-called hardship is purifying thru frequencies that can and will make people think differently. Change in your world is never easy, for your survival imprints hold on for desperation, for survival is mandatory."

"The City of Light designed in the current renovation of earth change will have people resting in the knowing that such a place has the ability to reconstruct much of the thinking from the old to the new; thus, healing will take place in each individual that will seem priceless, for there is nothing to compare it to."

"Someone has asked you recently about the current exchange of money. Money as such will become a thing of the past, just like stones were exchanged in the distant past and are no more, where much had to be stored for individual comfort of survival sake. This will become a mental opening of sharing instead of hoarding. This, of course, will take some time of exchange of thoughts and emotions, et cetera, but it has been said the new times of process and healing is Mandatory. The Money God will reign no more!"

"It will become people first. The changeover with them through a re-evaluation of their thinking and intent will be a major factor that puts new ideas into place. The necessity of change now runs rampant in fear like a virus that passes on from person to person through the media impact that is not a help but a hindrance. That is because negativity begets negativity and people have that already preset to continue more of the same. This is to be stopped, and the City manifestation will shake out a lot due to beliefs that God has indeed brought forth the manifestation of new life."

"You are a designated human who works to stay stable in the midst of the turbulence around. Some days are better than others when cooperation and love is felt as well as given, and love should lead the way. Now then what would you ask of us?"

GENII: "To keep me informed of what is in process and allow me more visits with questions as well as to continue to inspect the City and even find out more about your cosmic community worlds."

OOO-LON: "As agreed. As you can see and sense, this is just the first step as said previously. The wound must be cleansed before the healing can take place, for this time no Band-Aid approach will do."

"As countries begin to look at themselves, and others as themselves like looking into a mirror, this will begin the peace talks. Remember even the darkest of minds are being affected, thus bringing up what has been held in the deepest recesses of the subconscious, and thus making them a target of their own thinking. They do irrational horrifying things, and usually in the name of God or Allah. Such nonsense is to be no longer tolerated. This is not an overnight process but it will be completed, for this planet will survive. We have appeared to have this known and completed."

"We are from many cosmic community locations and galaxies, and this way of living on your planet affects the whole universal hologram. Nothing is separate, all is one. Every Light Being unseen, every star, every planet and much that you know not of, are all affected and subject to what this planet subscribes to. Every insect, flower, animal and tree plays a part in the holiness of what we are about."

"Some of your antics are deplorable and will be stopped! The make-up of your decisions will be changed one way or another. Since you cannot seem to do it easily, the community of universal helpers are on hand and have been for some time, and will continue to be to the finality."

"All the star riders, brothers and sisters have long since been evolved and involved as a vast community that recommends that the mind set of individuals here be changed to only know love for themselves, and respect of each other will be the healing process taking over."

GENII: "What about the individual health healings?"

OOO-LON: "What takes years and tons of money to find cures from cancer or some other self-induced appearance will be brought to a close, as the cure is known by the Star Community now! The hard part is in the human thinking, as they are used to being 'ill' and scarification comes from the inner voice of the subconscious that is a melody that repeats itself. When this is cured, the void could be a breeding place of something else. And the beat goes on. One has to be very strong not to accept an illness in any form."

GENII: "Like in my book The Sickness Bug, about addictions?"

OOO-LON: "The doctors and the forerunner scientists here are being guided to check new ways to cure old ways, but this is snail slow, which is fine for the pharmaceutical companies who make millions on its products. Again, the money god is mentally in charge. Why would they want people well? They have a surprise in store, believe it!"

"We are here to bring peace on earth, as has been the cry for centuries. This is in process, for the Universal Governing Light will have nothing less, so the cosmic community joined in to bring this about. First to find the power within themselves, then the planet's exterior by going into and through the people themselves."

"Consciousness must be raised, and the fantasy of love empowerment within each individual will make this a reality. Walk your day as one in Light, thus wherever you go or whomever you meet can have even a slight personal change that will benefit all. It is when you recognize and appreciate each other the changes happen, and quite quickly. A lifting this way is important. The new President called Obama knows this and is purposely put in this place of honor to recycle old thoughts into new ones as he attempts to instill this in others long since in old ways of thinking."

With this he sat down and another entity on his left side stood up, looked at me and said, "We are here to extend the holy way of cleansing through higher intelligence and shall be open to new questions as they come to mind."

He sat down and I was tapped on the shoulder by my Guide that it was time to depart. I thanked this cosmic council force for peace, stood up and was led out of the room with no walls, back to the Gate and then back home in Sedona, ready to see what today brings besides trying to type all this up!

So Light it be!

Somewhere in Non-Time

EMBASSY OF PEACE HEADQUARTERS February 20, 2009

As I release my physical world I seem to be soaring forward in time to begin my reentry into the City. My guide, La-Luke, waves as I land near him.

LA-LUKE: "Come. We go to the Embassy. You are expected."

The little wheel-less trolley waited as we moved through the park of relaxation and climbed aboard. This was a combination of sunlight and night. Strange, to be sure, but … well, I am in another dimension. The trolley (with no driver in sight) stopped. Things work differently in other dimensions. Are we way behind, I wondered.

As we entered this domain of light, all the entities around the table were standing, then they bowed in acknowledgement, which put me at ease. There was nothing like the pictures in the air that I had seen before, just faint, delicate fragrances lifting the senses, including my own. I found my chair and La-Luke stood next to it. I wondered what would happen next. I was soon to find out.

OOO-LON: "We welcome you back to the future."

I nodded in appreciation and mumbled, "Thank you."

OOO-LON: "There is a question for us?"

GENII: "Yes, a couple."

OOO-LON: "Proceed."

GENII: "In my own case, since all this is like a new adventure, what is God's highest vision for me in regards to the City demonstration?"

OOO-LON smiled, and that energy was picked up by the others. Not bad, looking at about nine entities all smiling at you.

GENII: "I have been on this path for some time watching and waiting like a spiritual detective for any clue that would give me advanced information as to what I call truth. And, what is to take place as I try to balance two worlds, one here and one in the physical? What am I to be advised to do to keep the process going and still take care of each physical day that appears at sunrise?"

OOO-LON: "You have spent much time in other worlds as you stretch forward in the imagination, which incidentally is where ideas are given to you by Intelligences of high order. Have you not been to the High Court? Have you been given emblems of healing use? Of course these are extensions of preparations you need as the forward push extends itself, as the Kathie has said with her channel session for you. How you relate to time is simply an effect, an end result, what you actually call truth. The message becomes decisive, thus elevating the mind and the physical space you occupy at this precise moment."

"Your body marks the advancement, as you are sensing energy patterns change within the cells and molecules, which is annoying at times. But this is necessary as even your senses elevate in experiencing this feeling of movement, all of which is in preparation of what is to come about. This will end. It was said before; this puts you up one more rung on the Light Ladder."

"Look at what is taking place. Do you note other dimensions and what you refer to as 'see-through' entities? Of course! Have you not asked to see the City entirety? Yes, of course you have. All is in divine order . All is applied as healing properties of advanced scientific design, and even you have just remarked that the moving picture of scientific value mixed with the spiritual is a concept you understand in your non-understanding."

"As has been said, as forward movement is applied to your senses, it will bring forth a cleansing so intense that all avenues you now work in will take second place (but they are important to the City demonstration). So in helping others such as children, you are preparing them also in your way to be able to handle the new world in process."

Of course we speak here of the puppets, as they are a valuable asset. So too are the women. You have not been given these tools to let them sit idly by. Use them to their highest advantage, now, as time, as you know it, is leaving and now-ness is put into action."

"Your earth collides within the new paradigm in process as your new President lays the ground work from two levels which he is programmed to do and has the courage to announce it to the world, ready or not, and is well able to take the kudos or the offence of misunderstanding. Where does he get his guidance? Does he not have spiritual guides of intelligence that tell him when and where to impress the public and has he not moved very quickly on that advice? You are seeing this take place, and all will in time be accepted. He moves mountains to make the little molehill, which people can climb over in their lives. He is clearing out and setting the course with the new thoughts being imbedded."

"The time will come when even you will speak on what this is all about and to him personally. Imagine that! Tis so…already done."

The spirit group around the table hummed in agreement as I sat wide-eyed in this declaration. Oh my....

GENII "And when will all this take place?"

OOO-LON: "Yesterday has left the experience and today is given credence to become more time of elevation and advancement. The changing of millions of minds to be on the same level takes various energy fields and much work for the same millions of spirit guides to reinforce the high level programming now in place. Finally this will and can take place."

"You say you are just one of those millions, but what has also been said is that it only takes one, and there are many more, including those who also related to the City of Light which also is energy in process with the thoughts and beliefs in place. Now as readjustments take place in your government systems, the flow will lift in acknowledgements that God has a direct plan of peace and love. The plan is brought closer as each day appears and the sun sets."

"We invite you here again to tell you and those asking questions that what has been previously said is activated, and the previous proclamation holds the power energy of truth. Take the wisdom and use it wisely."

"2012? We smile, as this date is not the beginning. It has long since begun. Enjoy the essence of this message, for God has power tucked in it. Come back with questions from others and yourself and we will set the answers in place, because intelligence moves forward with this guidance as all are reflections of the one, whole like a hologram. We bid you a peaceful loving day of physical existence. Peace be with you."

And with this La-Luke and I left the place of Light and went to the Gate of Entrance.

With my CD playing Somewhere in Time, I begin a new day here on this planet.

So Light It Be!

Of the President, Genii's Talents and Advancement

EMBASSY VISIT March 6, 2009

The vision scene opens as I ascend into it and arrive at the Gate of Welcome. It feels good to be back. Now where, I wondered. My guide La-Luke meets me and ushers me through the park of relaxation and onto the waiting floating trolley I have ridden on before.

GENII: "Where to?" I ask.

LA-LUKE: "We again enter the Embassy of Peace." The honor of being there brings forth to me respectfully more information and guidance. "They want to speak to you to further your course."

By the time this all was said, we had arrived at this magnificent building and I was ushered into this room filled with entities, and even the balcony appeared filled. It was much like an amphitheatre.

GENII: "My! Something must be important to bring forth such an audience," I whispered to my guide. He just smiled and nodded.

This room appeared much larger than before, and that was a surprise, but the horseshoe table with the leaders was the same. I curtsied and took a deep breath and La-Luke ushered me to the throne-like seat. Facing this vast audience was a thrill in itself.

The leader, OOO-LON, once again stood and a hush fell over everyone as if God itself was about to speak.

OOO-LON: "We welcome you back to our Sanctuary of Light. This, your return visit, has deep significance because the process of cleansing your planet has taken several steps forward through the inner directions given to the President of the name tone Obama."

"The flurry of dissention is only due to each one's personal memory, thus bringing forth the discomfort being experienced. Nevertheless the cleansing will continue, for each person must wash out in their own way, and that is what makes for the discomfort. Changes in frequencies is the key reason that moved heaven and earth into the process of moving heaven (so called) to earth."

"This tone has been sounded for centuries. The path of blame has always been put on God instead of where it belonged, or for the love of Allah one man kills another with no respect nor even knowing of that person. War will end!!!! Thus

Allah has decreed and peace remembered is all that will remain, as the pairs of opposites balance out, equal not in opposition but in love and caring. Harm is not the answer, love is! Make a note of this."

"What has been remarkable is that as more light enters and stirs up the pot, changing the old ways, we see love and caring for each other begin to take place as it should. This, then, gives our process a pathway of expression and correct solution."

"We here as Light Leaders in contact with other various planetary entities or groups make the light contact even here on your earth. This is intentional and will proceed to the finish, for as been said, THIS PLANET WILL BE HEALED!"

By this time I was certainly tuned in and turned on as I suspect these entities are visitors from outside our earth system. The power in that place is beyond awesome. There was total control...total!

OOO-LON: "With the support of those unseen in your dimensional world we have the continuing power to implant and sanctify what is being said and done. Today the main message is to share your given wisdom plus your varied talents as well as your love, thus leaving each person with a change for good in their own light. You have been chosen to move as much as possible into your world."

"Based on all of the above, the City Lights are magnified, so to speak, for your attention and acceptance. The Holiness of this awesome project cannot be emphasized enough and it bears witness to what is to come about . . . and soon."

"All the inner areas of process setting these healing facilities are in place, each one an entity within itself, thus energizing to reach out past dimension separation to draw to itself what it intends to accomplish in the near future."

"You have been given pages of writing describing what is unseen to the eyes of others. This is true, so you can carry in your heart and light body systems both a complete feeling and complete sight. This is purposely administered to you as an earth emissary of truth speaking, and will continue as you are moved from place to place and people to people to be contacted when and where advised. This City of Light demonstrates what God has decreed to be the fact and not fiction, and rightly so."

"The path before you periodically will lead you into new avenues and you can expect to have your name be very well known as the interest becomes fascinating to others. Make a mental note of this now, for the closeness of the demonstration appears on the horizon like the sun coming up over the red rocks that you love. Even the rocks have held power, along with the working vortexes that you are quite aware of."

"Your work in progress leaves you little time to influence the world at this time, as has been said of the President of the tone name of Obama connection, and how to be present in his presence has been outlined. The White House is by our estimation now called the Light House, and what does a Light House do for sea fearing travelers but be a beacon of comfort?"

I blinked and tried to think of something to say but a mental blank was what came up at this point.

GENII: "Well, what are my next closest steps advised?"

OOO-LON: "Be open to any opportunity that is advised. Make the days be filled with thoughts of the process of bringing forth The City. Head for the children and the women. Remember your talents where they would be appreciated with service given. Most of all, give love and a smile that could be worth a million to one who needs a smile at that moment."

"So now explore your new thoughts as they are introduced, and play in God's world, for it is your Playground of Progress just because you declared it to be so."

So Light It Be!

With that the scene ended and with no trolley I was just transported back to Sedona in thought.

Cosmic Dream Makers!

CITY EMBASSY VISIT April 10, 2010

As the entrance gate loomed large and beautiful before me in the sunlight, I have such a happy feeling that I almost run through it to get to the Park of Relaxation just beyond. It feels like spring time that bubbles up within me and I am happy to be here.

Into the park, I head for one of the massage benches located hither and yon. Oh my God this is sooo good! Looking around, my constant City Guide La-Luke settles beside me and I feel completed, honored and slightly wonder what is next?

"Embassy visit?" asks La-Luke. I smile as this is now, a favorite location and a place to see entities from various planetary locations. "Sure, let's go" I hear myself saying and smiling. Then we could hear the trolley slide up and we hopped aboard eager to get going. A short ride and here comes the Embassy and we unload at the huge doorway filled with flowered vines that smell delicious.

Inside, past the flowering foyer, the amphitheater had a hum-like sound as though many unknown languages were being spoken that came from many faintly-seen figures that filled the background. With the usual extra entities beside him, the head honcho OOO-LON stood, and from his sleeved robe held out his hand in welcome which was a first for me. It was usually just a bow. Ah, progress being made. I gladly took the offering which left me tingling from head to foot and then returned to my usual seat of some kind of honor.

OOO-LON spoke: "And what would be the purpose of your visit?"

Genii: "I am not sure; to learn more I suspect. What can you share with me that would be important to the world I am to share with?"

OOO-LON: "In the making of your new world, you know of the blessings to come forth as God empties the dark energies and as they rise to the surface to be acknowledged and then dissipated. In the wake of what is being done, we can tell you all is on course so, set you mind at ease. The past interest of the horror of the world's demise is looked upon as the totality of the apocalypse written so long ago. Not so."

"People read into that as all is lost and the end is near. Such nonsense. Why would God destroy what is a beautiful companion of its design to others in this holographic universe? Only ignorance stays in fear and actually thinking it is correct. We shake our heads in unbelief and in your words say 'this is dumb thinking' when taking the thinking of something holy and beautiful and healing is the total result. Please."

"So if the world empties itself of fear and ignorance what could be better? Darkness wants to stay that way and as the Light of the One penetrates this ignorance, it squirms in its losing power."

"Those who embody the cosmic areas of love penetration beget more of the same. That is the change and the END result. The building of the new earth, is a project of the Cosmic Dream Makers every one, and billions with them say 'YES THIS IS CORRECT!' You of planet Earth shall be a neighbor we are proud to sail through the universe with!"

"The cosmology of the planets and sub planets to bring forth the new birth of this planet that ignorance has almost destroyed, says that this planet and mother nature has decreed it will survive at all costs!"

"Ignorance and darkness of various kinds have held the reigns for far too long. The end is in sight for it no longer has a comfortable place to fester and cannot stand under the God Light now penetrating and rightly so. In meetings we have here, we share with you that the City of Love has given notice of its coming advancement and so it is!"

I tried to give some kind of remark or acknowledgement but the power I feel in this place keeps me in awe. I guess I would not care to be darkness of any kind. Wow!

OOO-LON continued: "Rest in the play of light and tolerate the darkness for yet awhile for, it is important for notification of the City and the uplifting value of those words you will speak. And so we rest this meeting."

In desiring to learn from the entities here of their origin, I sensed it could be arranged and we left the building and headed for the meeting Gate. I thanked my guide and even got a cosmic hug back...groovy! How blessed am I to be able to do, see and feel what is coming into form. And with that, I find myself back in Sedona on a sunny clear day knowing what I know for sure and this ends this Embassy visit.

Thanks God! It was a de-light!

So Light it be!

Betwixt And Between Earth Growth!

EMBASSY VISIT April 20, 2009

The Gate opens as I appear into the scene. I had received an invitation to return. My guide, La-Luke, also arrives at the same moment and beckons me to follow him. The trolley arrives to take us to the Building of Light Entities who hold a governing status previously seen where questions of the City and planet nature are discussed with authority as its main component.

Seeing familiar buildings again puts me into the mental framework that this production has more value than we could ever envision. The trolley stops at this Governing Building and we enter where we then face a multitude of entities in an amphitheater-type setting with many levels. As usual, the main unshaped table was hosted by the same entities holding court I had spoken with before. They now stood to greet me close up.

I was escorted to the throne-like chair. My guide stood beside me on my right. The leading major domo stood in his long white robe that seemed to glisten in the overhead daylight streaming in, while the others were seated. What an interesting place this is, I thought, as he began to speak.

OOO-LON: "We welcome you back and have a message that you are to take to your world. The patterns of change on your plant will continue for a bit yet, as the darkness has penetrated deep into the energy fields of the earth, so-called. The ground will heave up its matter as it maintains its process of loosing up or giving up its depleting energy now in release of the old. This may cause some traumatic movements as the earth breaths in the new in the release of the old."

"This information is not to frighten you but to make you aware and balance what is unbalanced, should it become apparent. You will know and be advised. The way presents itself, and as soon as it does, use what you are given while staying in an un-turmoil state of mind. Recognize that what is coming will take precedence of what may be important to you....first things first."

Genii: "You are speaking here of a vision I had some years ago of a major California coastline quake?"

OOO-LON: "Precisely, but even in other areas. The planet is a boiling pot of energy and predictions can become apparent at any time."

Genii: "I have another question. Charles Betterton has been highly trained in disaster areas procedures. Would this be a part of his journey?"

OOO-LON: "As said, 'previously trained in this kind of trauma, he would be called forth to assist in any area that has him so guided. Make each day a glossary of good tidings and accept as such."

"In the light of this place you are now visiting, come back as often as possible and in-between keep up your strength and endure your outside world. As the earth gives up its past history and thus brings forth the new, it has normal ways of doing this, either in human form or by earth shudders. So then, be of light cheer, for more is to be explored."

And with that my guide nodded to me to rise, as the entities also did, and bowed, and we were excused to leave the building. We took the waiting trolley to the Gate as La-Luke smiled at me.

Then the whole scene disappeared as I find myself back in Sedona, thankful for the opportunities afforded me to enter into the unseen to explain this to whoever is tuned in.

So Light it be!

Energy Healing With Genii and Roger

EMBASSY VISIT May12, 2010

I am excited to see what can take place with Roger Dycaza, as he enters the City for the first time after being invited to the Embassy, where I have never taken anyone before. My envision showed that we and many others were also entering. One look at smiling Roger told me he had found the reason for his transmission healing work. Yes, this was it; the reason for it all.

Suddenly La-Luke appeared and tapped Roger on the shoulder startling him a bit. They introduced themselves as we entered through the encoded entrance.

Roger was grinning trying to take this all in. "'This is magnificent" he muttered. Then it was into the park of relaxation where he got his first taste of what a massage bench was for as he relaxed on one.

La-Luke motioned that the wheel-less trolley to the Embassy was waiting. The trolley waited patiently as we three climbed aboard, tipping it a bit on its nothing underpinnings, and then zoom … we literally flew over the ground. Roger tried to take in all the buildings we passed and before long we were in front of the beautiful Embassy building entrance while Roger tried not to miss anything.

The melt-through doors brought us into the lush gardens and the beauty to be enjoyed. That was followed quickly by being led into the main chamber that held hundreds of beings (most not seen but surely felt) headed up by 5 entities at the main table in front of us. The center speaker was OOO-LON, whom I have met here many times ... a male light filled with such love and wisdom that it can take one's breath away. How blessed we are to be in his presence.

My usual throne-type chair now had one more added for Roger. He took a deep breath, trying to believe all that he was seeing, and wondering what or who he was not privy to see in the rear audience. But there was no doubt that there were plenty of beings here, believe you me. We were escorted to our chairs where we were seated and acknowledged.

OOO-LON: "We see you have fulfilled your mission with the dark haired human. Sir you work with the humanoids. You can be readied to help them even more as you now have direct contact with the 'ENERGISTS' of space content. High esteem beyond your earth channel ways. Your work so far has the imprint of what has healing effects; is this true?"

Roger worked hard in this scene to get the word 'yes' out. It was clear to see he was overwhelmed with what is taking place as well he should be. I know.

Talking about a 'City' to appear out of nowhere is one thing, but actually being in it is another, and then having a space person ask him a question was almost too much on a first visit.

OOO-LON continued," So you would be willing to have an expert scientific cosmic teacher show you how to use what you have and add even more?"

Roger nodded his head, said "Yes" and that he would be honored.

OOO-LON: "Good then, meet your space teacher of 'EMORGY'. It is advanced energy."

Appearing from his left side, an entity stepped forward. The appearance was of an aged man with many wrinkles, but with eyes that shone like spotlights in the dark, and his face shone, as well as his silver blue 2-piece suit and boots to match. This was quite an entity I thought, but I am getting used to everything being different. This one is indeed pure light!

He spoke and in our language "My tone name is. YA-FU-FUS, but you may call me 'YA'. I speak in your tongue. You speak space?"

Roger shook his head no.

YA continued, "YA will suffice. I will speak in 'EMORGY' tone for understanding. As the 'EMORGY' comes to you, the understanding will too." At this point I thought I might have to pick Roger off the floor, but it proved that was not necessary. I asked him if he was all right and he answered "Yes, just amazed."

YA: "Then new student, this is how we shall begin. When you go in to your quiet space of meditation I shall send you messages through this new energy system, so it is important that you be open to receive and record what is transferred to you. Keep a record somehow of what is said. You understand YA?"

Roger: "How often will these transmissions come?"

YA: "You will know when they arrive. Take time out to receive. Picture the vision taking place right now as I am speaking with you and the transmission information shall begin for note taking. Don't get frustrated or worried as this may take a few YA visits to set your mental course, you understand?"

Roger: "Yes, I look forward to being able to learn more. Thank you. Thank you."

YA: "Any more questions?"

Roger: "No, I have to digest all this I guess. It is a bit overwhelming and on such a grand scale. Amazing!"

And with this YA bowed, turned and left the scene with a murmur coming from the unseen audience.

OOO-LON: "As for the Genii … stay open. Your changes come in quickly. Be the light you are and we shall rest in the wisdom of your knowing."

La-Luke motioned us it was time to leave and we did after acknowledging the leaders, and we headed for the door, the trolley, the park and the gate.

With a hug from Roger and La-Luke, I found myself back sitting in a car somewhere in Cottonwood, Arizona waiting for Charles to come back from his visit with new friends.

And that is the beginning of a new story for Roger.

So Light it be!

A Time for Light

EMBASSY VISIT May 26, 2009

My destination was the Embassy of Peace and I wondered what would take place within this amphitheater of cosmic visionaries who also gather there, headed up by several who speak with me from a place of power and love. I wondered what to ask as we entered. Maybe nothing? Maybe just listen and absorb? The collection of cosmic minds inside was consciousness at its highest peak so I had a curiosity and expectancy for what would take place.

As we entered there was indeed the sensing of much power and love mixed like a delicious concoction. Once more I recognized OOO-LON, the leading speaker, as I was led to the throne-type chair as before.

OOO-LON rose and spoke, "Welcome to the assembly of Cosmic Intenders. How may we serve you?"

I gulped, as I had no real question, just what I had been thinking about the 2012 date line.

OOO-LON spoke again. "We detect your interest in a dateline that could be a target of that interest, so permit us to gather in combined thought and answer."

For a moment or two there was total, really total silence; not a breath was heard. There must have been hundreds of entities in this arena who all stopped breathing at the same moment, or at least it seemed that way, like all thoughts had stopped the clock. Clock? What's a clock? It felt like nothing, a void, a moment in time. What is time? A connecting of mental oneness that we don't experience normally. The message was clear.

Then, as if someone turned on a switch for God to begin again, these entities that I sensed came from some far off cosmic community returned from wherever they went in those few moments. My guide smiled down at me from where he stood beside me.

OOO-LON continued: "Dates are man's way of keeping time in constant continuum for various reasons unique to themselves. Perhaps to put progress on the calendar, it is useful. The silence you have just witnessed gives invitation to the non verbal that you have not asked. In the case of the City appearance, we smile at all the delights to be seen and experienced as this demonstration is set before you."

"As the current light waves move all into place so people can see what you have been shown so far, it is magnificence as if heaven on earth has landed. And God had said, 'Let there be Light, and a City of Light to attest that indeed I exist, and I as the Primal Source of all things visible and non-visible bring it all forth: the biggest gift ever given any place.' It is time this planet interacts with other cosmic communities!"

"Those seated here are from such communities, each bringing forth their Light intelligence into the formation of what can be accomplished as this prototype City of Light demonstrates on this planet."

"Those who see, let them see those who are connected, due to the information they have recorded as preconceived through this visioning you are sharing, and many other ways unique to themselves as valid. All are connected as such; same time line, same space station."

"The attraction here is the healing facilities that can get the job done in a compressed time awareness. All appearances are illusions of the mind, and thus light illusions can heal what most do not understand, and they will, for here there is no discrepancy, it just is! Much has been used and approved in many cosmic universal universities that are not known of."

"2010, 2011, 2012. This time has been predicted through high clear minds, and many demented minds as well. Which do you choose? These higher forms have given you what you have attested to through many visits here and many more to be addressed. So, then, leave us and reenter into your world and testify what is coming about, for indeed it is so!"

"Recognize what is happening here is that your contact with the cosmic community is established and will be of good use because you will be invited to enter and view this cosmic community. As has been said, welcome to your future, welcome to journeys beyond space!"

And as he said this, all the entities stood up and sounded some unknown tone, and with that La-Luke tapped me on the shoulder and I knew this session, with all that had been said, was definitely very over.

From Time to Time

EMBASSY OF PEACE VISIT June 7, 2009

Being able to envision the most awesomely beautiful where the technology is superb beyond our knowing now and the healings complete, is a gift that only God could imagine. This is the revelation that is at hand. Imagine that!

Resting in this awareness, I find myself back at the now familiar gate of entrance into the abode God has brought forth, at least at this point in my inner vision. High above me I look at this gold-encoded design circling the open horseshoe shape open entrance and I wonder at the magic of it all; untested in our world to be sure, but surly magical in the intent of a healing place long past due.

Lightworkers have had visions of what is to come about and have tagged 2012 as some kind of appointment, like expecting the Christ or Buddha or whomever to come into view. Hey ... with God all things are possible, right?

That brings me to my question: Why me? A high school drop-out who could only utter a few words due to stuttering. Maybe Moses said the same thing as he was told to talk to the Pharaoh and he stuttered, it is reported. I know the feeling!

Here I stand on holy ground looking at the gateway of advanced progress that I am to talk about to others. Who would have thought? Not me. This is so far from my imagination that ...oops... I feel a tap on my shoulder and I turn to see my City Guide La-Luke smiling at me and moving me through the archway entrance.

"Where are we going? " I enquired, still in the mental magic of it all.

LA-LUKE: "To the Embassy of Peace!" And with that the wheel-less trolley pulled up and we climbed aboard. It took no time before we were unloaded at this Temple of Light. We entered to find this amphitheater filled to overflowing with entities from cosmic locations of some place. The scene repeated itself as I was ushered to the seat of visitors as a seat of honor.

OOO-LON: "Welcome to the next step of your advancement. How may we serve you?"

GENII: "I am looking for answers to questions I do not even know to ask. Does this make any sense?"

OOO-LON smiled slightly. "Questions of the City Intent have been explored and 'timing' of this event seems to be on your mind. Is this so?"

GENII: "People are looking to 2012 as a date of something to take place, but most are not sure of what it is. Can you tell me what is to take place that has far reaching effects before that calendar date 2012? We are almost there."

A hum ran through the almost invisible audience.

OOO-LON: "The world of the planet has yet a bit of time for the change, due to the light waves washing the outer and inner interiors, much like washing a window so you can see clearer. Layer after layer of darkness is being removed not only from each person but the naturalness of the planet itself, as the new course is set into place."

"I am sure you are aware of the centuries of wars that have contributed from the darkness of the minds corrupt in ego fears to these layers being cemented. The minds of the people of all races need to be lifted by these changes, and now quickly, as the energies push out the old and in with the new."

"You can expect this to continue, and by the end of 2010 much of this will be a whole course of action and accepted by many. The topsy turvey roller coaster example is in full force now, making people misjudge due to their own discomfort, but they will continue never-the less, as people must confront their own insecurities. In doing so they lash out at others as a mirrored effect instead of what you call 'going with the flow.' All this drama of release attracts the earth changes as well."

"Hurricanes, tornados and quakes, which are all energy induced with these cleansing techniques, can be seen as possibly traumatic. People have to handle this as weather changes as well. The old ways of doing things that impeach others not at the highest will find no place in your society. Love and honor will replace greed and personal salvation for themselves only will take a back seat of resolution declaring 'no more!'"

"The Light attends all who love and will dramatically affect these encounters. The unseen visionaries who work in the unseen higher realms forge health and happiness for all. The wars of greed will fall away, for all will be established as a norm."

"First the first...cleansing at all costs! Those who are in the government themselves are in their own process to lead through the next two years of the date you have been speaking of, but remember what you call time as a no thing is collapsing and 2012 may well be 2010. This was said to you earlier, that they were not considering time collapsing when these dates were given so long ago in ancient times."

"So then what are you to do in the meantime?

    1. Listen for guidance every step.

    2. Stay in the openness of what may be shown and said.

    3. Watch for the unsettlement which will continue more of the same for awhile yet.

    4. Do not get caught up in it, even with those you love.

    5. Your course is set! Stay there.

    6. Watch your interests change as you move forward.

"Any more unknown questions?"

GENII: "My senses tell me to just embody what you have said as a confirmation. More about the 'new course' would be helpful."

OOO-LON: "Now that we have laid the ground work, be open to the new course and ideas to be implanted. As the new imagination shifts, implants of the new will be accepted as such. Add the new chapters to the book so all is kept in chronological order. This will be important as the questions come forth and you have a solid reply!"

La-Luke tapped me on the shoulder and I recognized my no-time session was up. I bowed to these leaders of leaders and turned to leave, at which time a hum again was heard somewhere in the audience. I bowed a thank you to the audience and my teachers in front of me. What an adventure I have tuned into. I realize that this is not my last visit, and I am so blessed.

Then it was back to the trolley, gate, and thanking La-Luke as I prepared to be home again in Sedona, Arizona to reread what I have written, because at this point I have not much of a memory of it.

So Light It Be

The Light of Interest

EMBASSY VISIT July 24, 2010

Another time another place, another dimension, but a place of such magnificence that seems to take my breath away every time I come back through my inner vision. I accept my visitation rights of City entrance and headed for the Embassy of Peace, beginning at the coded gate of entrance, where my City guide La-Luke greets me with a hug.

Grabbing my hand, we ran through the Park of Relaxation and onto the waiting driver-less, wheel-less trolley that skims over the ground with us aboard. I can assume that there are many of these trolleys taking people from place to place within the City interior, but so far this is the only one I have seen. This huge almost egg-shaped building holds an entrance garden with fragrances that bring such peace that it seems to set the scene for this Embassy of Peace.

Once more inside this main sanctuary, I see the 5 cosmic CEO's sitting at the front table and hear the vast unseen, but felt, audience of hundreds of entities. Some were behind them. They stand in a bowing welcome and look to my seating in the usual high-back chair where La-Luke leads me.

It is an honor to be here … no doubt of that! The leader OOO-LON, speaker of space and human's language, spoke in our language for my understanding.

OOO-LON: "We welcome the Genii back. How may we be of service?"

GENII: "I come for:

1. Any advisement on my future steps,

2. To learn more of speaking space and

3. A student/friend has requested a question and answer session. He is considered a C-L, 'City Light' and he is dedicated to service for the City. I have asked him to report his needs."

OOO-LON: "Proceed."

GENII: "This is his report/question, as given him by his inner 4 Keys guide MAR-EEK:

From William Henry Barton IV … How shall I best serve and be of service while in a state of surrender to the City of Light, keeping in mind and being aware of the fact that my inherent gifts from God include a continuous powerful, and abundant flow of live force energy (Chi) throughout my being, as well as having a particularly close connection with electricity and/or energy generation. Thank You."

OOO-LON: "It would be wise to share with this human male, that he has yet another guide with whom he can accelerate in the areas of his speaking and the learning therein. The City of Light, as this male knows, is electrically enhanced with such power that is not known to people on your planet."

"As you would say, the power within it is awesome from the High Towers collection of the UPPCs to the under-City electromagnetic fields and computers beneath, reporting on what is happening above. All is electrified to the point of even sending energy to other states in need. Now then, from his Soul Light Guide, The William can get precise instruction pertaining to his part in the mechanics of the electronics pertained to in the message to him."

"As he leads himself under this guidance, he can become an intricate part of the over-all picture and be able to answer questions from others as a teacher/leader would, as you are doing now."

"His Soul Guide teacher does "Speak Space" and also his English as you understand. But he brings the Light electrified into the planet to maximize the power this planet needs to overcome the low consciousness spoken of many times. ZOOO-NAAR is this guide and a master in these fields and quite open to instruct The William further."

At this point a hum of acknowledgment sounded in the audience, and the head CEO's nodded Yes…

GENII: "Will William be guided step by step so he can also teach and give information to further the interest in the City construction in printed data for City books etc.?"

OOO-LON: "Quite so. With his intent of service to the City manifestation and being open to his City Guide."

(NOTE: Each human that has been 4 Keys linked has a "City" Guide who will instruct the talents of that individual who wants to be of service using them, and can be so intoned.)

"You have been given the title of 'Advanced Achievement Academy' (AAA) connected to the Light Center. Report these findings and recognize that pods of information can be given of this advancement as they, as their soul teachers in human form, lead the way as experts in action."

GENII: "Thank You. I will pass this information on to others as well."

OOO-LON: "And now then . . . The Genii has been into the advancement of moving the City data from her house to the White House. This will continue to completion! The path ahead we seek to see you complete as doors with Light intent open before you. Make note of the advancement. Your path is secure and the target dates will appear like magic. Just hold the Light forward and expect the unexpected in delightful ways" He says as he smiles and nods in agreement.

"Your visit here today has been of great value to others. The gifts of the fun of strings and things have been a value to yourself and others. Yes, you have served in many ways. Now then, take a bit of time to enjoy what you enjoy for smiles and laughter is indeed healing. Take your gifts of fun and just give them away. This is your time … and God agrees."

"Be of good cheer. All is well and on course. We shall attend to more again on your next visit."

"We see that your energy is getting low." With that they all stood, smiled and bowed as La-Luke and I did the same and we headed for the doorway, the trolley and the gate, and I now find myself home with my furry white pup 'Light Spirit' wanting some fun.

So Light It Be.

The Big One!

EMBASSY VISIT August 6, 2009

Closing my eyes and moving in an inner vision to another place of familiarity, I find myself again at the Entrance Gate into the City of Light. My visits have been numerous and I now can add yet another one, this one, a request to return from inside the City.

A Gate of Entrance once more beckons me to enter. No one else was seen who had been seen before on several occasions. I was apparently quite alone, but no, my City guide, La-Luke, appeared as if by magic and led me through the five story entrance building.

How blessed I felt knowing that I was in God's favor. The familiar Resting Park came into view, but no stopping to rest on a groovy massage bench this time. Pulling aside the giant willow-like curtains, we hopped aboard the familiar wheel-less trolley that whisked us off to the Embassy of Light. This building holds the Power of the Universe, due to the Entities seated within sharing love and information with energies not explainable. It is just that strong.

Having been summoned to return here I wondered why? Do I have any questions? Well, one for sure, having just been told by Archangel Michael through a human channel by two friends who shared with us that a "Big One" earth-wise is to be experienced. What is the big one and how does it affect us?

The trolley stopped and we entered this hall of magnificence and awesome power mixed with love unimaginable ... Oh my God! The entities of this place stood and nodded while I was escorted to my now usual throne-type chair. A hum went through this extra large light arena, with Lord knows how many entitles filling every seat in this vast audience that was unseen but surely felt.

OOO-LON, the leader began, "We welcome you back to this place of light for a particular reason, which you have already been given in what you would call a clue. Your earth patterns are shaping up to bring forth a massive undertaking of change. This will, by no means, be just a small indication of what is to come. It has already been triggered."

"These things that have and are taking place are true in the eyes of Archangel Michael, for he makes his words through another human to take note of what to be aware of, not in fear but in preparation to take on any situation that appears unusual. This, then, would be a confirmation of same. So then what to do?"

"Stay in the love that accompanies and know that this is all love directed and not fear based, that people of your dimension will do it on their own. Take each day as a celebration to honor that God of Light that will soon ascend onto the planet in a different form than human to be sure, but yet the same."

"Star workers set in motion what needs to be put into action to lift those who second guess this change of frequencies. This Embassy makes the world sacred in its dealings in and of this planet, and in doing so, makes its graduation, so to speak."

"Gathered in this Embassy are Light Beings from around the Galaxy, and in themselves just being here cross-over changes are being made. This cosmic community intersects with the world dimension you live and function in. It takes massive attention gesturers to bring people together as one in the love and light of what this City represents totally."

"So then, as when any change appears, fear comes as a companion rushing forth to protect in the survival system programmed within. People fear what is unknown or not understood, but for some, they move through that into higher knowing that 'all is well'."

"The energy patterns of change are moving into 'shock' position and all will feel the impact. Due to the inner feelings of light workers, a knowing is produced even before it is validated by your media. When the inner terror raises to be experienced as a disaster, to those who have been elevated in consciousness to a higher point of understanding they know that the necessity to cleanse is the perfect recognition of what is taking place and all in divine right order. Do you understand these words?"

GENII: "Yes, and what would be our position to move through such an earth-changing unsettling trauma?"

OOO-LON: "Practice staying in balance in the knowing of what is to be brought forth, and that the City of Light has been selected to bring such healings that have never been seen before on this planet. It has been said before that the City of Light has been selected to bring forth healings and would be a major attention-getter, never before produced or seen in your world. To have a trauma happen, it then becomes validated and the imprint is very effective, because then people believe their prayers are being answered, through the combined energy of the City. And they trust in God, Buddha or whomever and say, 'Yes, they have appeared to help us, praise God!'"

"This precursor to the City is in place. An example would be that this planet would be like a dog shaking off water from his fur. Trauma brings people together in loving ways and shakes off the darkness of undeveloped light. Those who cannot hold such energy patterns will leave and only return when they decide to learn the 'light way'.

"So then, this gathering is a preview of what was announced eons ago and mentally programmed as 'The Big One.' Prepare not for fear, but in the holy revelation that the Christ principal is in action and the Genii remembers the old song title 'On that great, come and get it day' and that will be when this planet shines in the heavens for all to enjoy near and far, never again to be destructive in its dealings."

"This City is a gift and all will know when it is time. Any more questions?"

GENII: "What is my passion in all this?"

OOO-LON: "Precisely why you are being advised to take the lead and be an example. Stay in your upper leveling and lift those who may not understand what is taking place. Meditate, rest, trans-audio, for your senses are becoming more refined as each moment passes. The world of illusion is in such a state of flux that it is important to bring forth the City of Light healing facility, and come it will! Now. have you received the impact of these words?"

GENII: "Oh my, yes. Being inside this City and its healing factors I know this is really needed, having been blessed to re-enter many times. Thank you for this magnificent dwelling of love that was delivered to Dr. Townsend so many years ago. I proudly carry on his legacy the best I can and will continue as advised and guided."

With this I knew my time was up, so I was escorted out of the building, on to the trolley and back at the Gate. I said goodbye to my guide and found myself back in my bed in Sedona on a sunny morning.

Contact!

EMBASSY VISIT, August 12, 2010

Resting in the knowingness of God, I mentally and visually head back into the City with the Embassy as my target. No gate or trolley is seen, much less my Guide this time. In vision I find myself standing in front of the 5 entities I have seen before as OOO-LON stands in bowed greeting.

Why did I decide to come today? No questions come to mind although I feel pretty balanced but floaty. Anyway here I am, somewhere in light.

OOO-LON: "You are confused?"

Genii: "No, I just came so quickly unprepared ... no questions except maybe, how can I be more supportive with the City demonstration?"

OOO-LON: "What more would you like to do?"

Genii: "First I would like to be more balanced physically in this unbalanced world. This is a nuisance."

OOO-LON: "You must recognize that in your mission, the changes within your system are taking on a major upheaval to bring you up to code so to speak. You can still function? "

Genii: "Oh yes, just a little lop-sided when walking sometimes and the spinning vortexes here in Sedona are not much help."

OOO-LON: "This is unavoidable at this time. Just be easy with it. Your earth world takes on a new glow and that in itself is uplifting, however strange and you are making the best of it all and actually moving yourself beyond where you have ever been before."

Genii: "Am I to meet more intelligences from space?"

OOO-LON: "Oh my yes, you have only begun to space walk and talk. Remember the Cosmic Collage you have had spoken of?"

Genii: "Yes."

OOO-LON: "Good, then we will bring forth a Space teacher who will direct your course."

Then entering from stage left is an entity that looks like a very bent over old man, gray beard covering part of his face but, still looking very young like a cocoon of light of some kind was around him. Hard to describe. He was so light.

How can this be? Am I imagining this as a 2 dimensional figure, like someone had put a curse on him like in beauty and the beast? He just kind of pulsated as waves of light surrounded him. Amazing! He was headed for me, uplifting anyone I bet who would be around.

OOO-LON: "It is important in your growth that you get used to light changes within an entity for, these are frequencies you can see, not all is solid. Meet your new space teacher. TWA-WAN and he can understand in your language."

Genii: "Hello" I weakly say, eyes wide open.

Twa-Wan: " Ahsseeee>>>>>>>>>" came a very elongated sound.

OOO-LON: "This may take a bit of time but he will interpret your sounds."

Genii: "Wow… this intelligence is a power house. Can I handle his energy?"

OOO-LON: "Think on this in the quiet of your home. Information will begin to float through to you."

Twa-Wan: "Saaaa>>>>>>>>>>>>>>>>>>>>>>>>>>"?

Genii: "OK, I get the picture. Twa-Wan I am pleased to meet you. You teach me to speak space?"

Twa-Wan: "Saaa >>>>>>>>"

Genii: "Why would I need to learn Space Sounds and what does this have to do with the City demonstration?"

OOO-LON: "Much, for in the Space Community you are able to understand those cosmic entities you will meet that are in the cosmic level of the City of Light. For now, just absorb what has just taken place. Bring more questions and again watch the film 'CONTACT' as it has vibrational sounds within the sound tract that will begin to resonate with you. Take your time, relax, rest and enjoy this newness."

And with this the Entity smiled and began to back off, both of him the old and the new. I felt the energy of this meeting was right on track.

If I had more questions, they left with the waves of frequencies being produced as I witnessed, and now as the vibration began to lessen, I feel it is time for Genii to go home and I do.

New day … puppy play and what the day will bring. Thanks God. I must have done something right to meet friends in very high places I never would have met any other way. I bless the City of Light and look to more power-filled meetings as the City appears as if by magic. So light it be!

Out With the Old And In With the New

EMBASSY OF PEACE HEADQUARTERS VISIT, August 27, 2009

In my vision I meet with my guide, La-Luke, at the now familiar Gate of Entrance into the City. We move through the Park of Relaxation on the wheel-less trolley heading for the Embassy of Peace where this immaculately-styled building holds many entities from the universe.

In entering I do recognize the Head Representatives of Information and OOO-LON, who is the only one so far that converses with me. A hush falls over all of them in the auditorium. As I sit down, he begins to speak in English.

OOO-LON: "You have arrived back with questions?"

GENII: "Yes, at least one!"

OOO-LON: "You are welcome, oh human leader of earth time, and your question is?"

GENII: Having a feeling he already knew, I proceeded anyway. "What update can you give me of the City's actual appearance that I can report, if the question is not out of line, please?"

OOO-LON smiled, as did several around this table of information. "As you embark to speak to many, it is noted since you are into space-time you request an update and this is unavoidable due to the inquiries coming from you and others. So then put this information on your sheet of advancement for City recognition."

"It is observed that your planetary objective is in two parts. One wants peace at all costs, the other peace at their own personal interests. The turmoil and unrest vacillates daily. The wars continue, and many have taken their place in their own ecstasy of killing. Sound strange? Programmed achievement here."

"The so-called Money God runs first with the Sex God coming in second, which in many cases are one and the same. This is noted as each individual has their own short comings, so called, to be cleansed. Are you getting the picture here?"

"The light waves now in process leave no personage out. All are in a major process of inner cleansing due to the new energy patterns being introduced, and massive changes are taking place. This cannot be avoided if the process is to be finalized."

"Thus, this massive endeavor brings to full view the City of Light."

"Strange feelings will be felt within each one occasionally not considered as normal, (The Genii will testify to this), inviting that person to re-evaluate what they are doing or have done in the past, as the mental upheaval will search for the answers."

"As has been said, your history will be just that, history of old doings, and this will dissolve in the ashes of the new births. People hold on to the old as the good old days. Well, they may not have been so good one way or another, but this still offers no advancement now unless some learning has come from it."

"It has done what it did then and now you are here, ready or not. The world unseen prepares for the City of Light, and it is like parting the seas, for it comes ready for action. So the update is all in order and moving into place. This is good news in the vastness of the universe. We who re-enter the wave of lingering earth thoughts seeking change which, as has been said many times, is in process."

"Take your given message to the world and those who seek answers will find this a step in the right direction. Be one who Lights their paths, for all it takes is one."

"Thank you for coming." And with that, OOO-LON sat down.

I bowed in thanks and La-Luke and I made our way to the exit, the trolley and the gate. I hugged my Guide of so many visits and the scene disappeared as I recognized the Sedona red rocks back home.

So Light It Be!

Of Upheaval and Staying Balanced

EMBASSY VISIT, September 11, 2009

The gate entrance was wide open as I entered the scene screen. La-Luke spread his arms open and grabbed my hand as we almost ran thru the park and on to the trolley which usually takes us to the Embassy of Peace Headquarters, and this time was no exception.

This short ride stopped at the Embassy entrance and we moved into this building of Light Entities. Total silence greeted us; not even a breath was heard from the hundreds of entitles who also filled this amphitheatre.

Nodding I smiled as I crossed in front of several governing leaders to my usual seating place. A nodding welcome was returned.

OOO-LON: "You have been quietly summoned here this morning for reasons of advancement. So we speak from a light heart."

"The world of human affairs lifts its angry head in protest of changes in process that now do not fit with the past old patterns. The change of energies plays havoc to many who are unaware of what is underlying this process, if indeed they know that a process is in process."

"It is important that you in particular know and recognize the value of what is taking place. For the most part you have been well informed, as you meet every challenge put to you in your own personal change-over."

"We are aware of the swiftness of each emotion that hits without warning on a continual basis. This restructure of your systems is important as you lead yourself to be much more than you have been in any lifetime. All this was to bring you to this point, this time, this moment, this century in history which coincides with the City appearance, for the intelligence energy patterns residing in your light body aura may speak to the masses of what is taking place."

"When you speak even now, one or more Intelligences may roar out the message of love to be sure, but direction to what is coming about is fact not fiction, and you feel the power within."

"Your system can shift many times in a period of one day. This you have felt from the highest touch of God to the lowest of being nothing."

"To stay in harmony it is important to have short periods of rest because the chemical make-up of your system is adjusting its alchemy patterns and the swing is not so harsh. So then what can be added?"

GENII: "Speak, please, of this country's governing forces and how I should look at this chaotic upheaval, the President and the City of Light appearance."

OOO-LON: "The determination that this country is for the people and one with God is primary, and nothing less will be tolerated. The Obama leader stands as a pillar of light that can withstand the harshness of the place he leads, and indeed all will be well and he and his family are well protected from the onslaught of viciousness of darkened minds who would themselves be in control."

"Adjustments are in process, so be it known that that the City of Light, in its place of being unseen at the moment, is waiting its appearance. Your place and those who also walk this path close to you are affected and admonished to keep the God intent as energies of honor. Stay the course, be the light and you all will make daylight out of darkness. We send you forth to release what is to be 'no more.'"

"The message you received to be able to see the City through human daily eyes in the physical will come as a see-thru advantage point and the validation therein. Stay on course as both you and the sister of lives past Kathie are predestined to attend the appearance."

"The Charles has his work cut out in blueprint for him in areas yet attracted but escalating him as Ambassador of World Green. So then this all being said, as you travel together to various places your Light intensive breaks forth any concerns anyone might have as he works to fulfill his destiny which, of course, connects to the City appearance."

"So then what say you?"

GENII: "My request is assistance to keep me balanced in the City Light, that my body keeps in its healthiness and my mind tuned into the frequencies of the City."

OOO-LON: "It is so advised! Now take yourself back to the physical and assist in cheer, love and peace and return as requested."

With that he stood and bowed as we left, heading back to the Gate. The scene vanished and I am back in Sedona to take care of my puppy that needed attention.

Today is the Tomorrow of Yesterday

EMBASSY VISIT, October 4, 2009

QUESTION: "What is to be known?"

ANSWER; "Nearer my God to thee brings forth the inner feelings of the Genii and touches her heart as she moves forward with her soul convictions of what is to come about in your dimension."

"The message is clearly defined in each contact, so permit us once again to have you enter into the sanctuary of peace and light, the City of God, which is opened to be entered into and enjoyed. As the coming prospects of it enter into your mental equation of life, it appears that that which is today is only the tomorrow of yesterday."

As I enter into my inner vision corridor, I see myself walking up to the golden awesome Gate, which is one of several and there are what look like crowds of people already there. They fade away, and my guide, La-Luke, smiles as I draw near and it all seems like a dream sequence. La-Luke holds out his hand as he smiles to see me.

LA-LUKE: "You have been away a long time." (It didn't seem like it to me, but what is time but an illusion anyway?)

Entering into the now familiar Park of Relaxation I was tempted to sit on one of the massage benches and do just that, enjoy the fantastic flowers, trees and just the peace of this place, but this was not to be our stopping place. As the wheel-less trolley pulls up I know that we are headed to the City Embassy of Peace a distance away.

We were hustled into the interior, which is like an amphitheatre with hundreds of entities in the background and several leaders who hold court (so to speak) around a horseshoe type table. I nodded and sort of bowed to those there as I was guided to the seat of honor (not sure what the honor is but it is comfortable and opulent so what is to be rejected?)

The leader, OOO-LON, stood and said, "You have had the feeling to return, is that not so?"

"Yes", I replied.

OOO-LON: "And so it is, and we welcome you on behalf of all in attendance here, many of whom are from other parts of the galaxy. They have been instrumental in putting forth this City you are speaking of to those who will listen."

"Is there a particular reason?" I asked.

"Quite so", he replied. "The terrain of the earth is in movement and various regions are and will be touched and evacuated due to the inner earth pressures of the new life changes in accordance with the coming of this holy place of healing. When fear is triggered, people look to God to save them from death, which leads them to God in any case."

"As the next advanced year enters the orbit, it is most important what has been revealed to you regarding the City. Stay in touch with the solid notion that the divine entrance will be of valued constructions being put into place and into the third dimension. All is on course."

"Forget not your position in the announcement of this heaven on earth, which has been pronounced for eons of time. And as repeated, this is the only one, a prototype that will be seen and be able to be entered into while the unseen ones are in place. It takes only one demonstration to shake up a world ready for healing. This is where you come into play."

"With the new paradigm now in effect, more teachers, channels and sight facilitators are desired to bring advanced awareness to the masses, so Lightworker attention should be put into place to teach the 4 Keys and Light Link to open the unknown light corridor and thus bring through their own personal soul guides and gatekeepers, as teachers and leaders will clear the way for the 5th Key. They will then enter the City personally to see for themselves what is coming about in this healing edifice."

"The closed holy door of the past is now opening for the Genii to teach the teachers, for time is short, so to speak. There are many who would be excellent leaders and can gather in their world many who can become the spreader of the news thru their own inner visits."

"To name a few who have been linked, Kathie Brodie, Richard La Duke, Renee Tendra, and even now a new friend of channeled masters Cynthia Williams who would be an excellent teacher since she is a noted channel herself. Plus there are more yet unknown."

"So then it is time to spread the word and pass the 4 Keys to Light on to others so they can link in light yet many more. What has taken four hours to teach the Keys now will be designed for approximately an hour or a bit more. A prepared session can be set in place in writing format and live action."

"How is this to be done, especially the hidden Word?" I asked.

OOO-LON: "Would we not explain this in its perfect order? Of course. More and more people are being open to receive unusual answers through their own light work, and the time is now. Travel is indicated, and even classes on the Internet can be programmed. Being open to the suggestions offered would be a part The Charles could lead in the way best expressed."

GENII: "And what of the personal guides and gatekeepers of each?"

OOO-LON: "Once the concept is in place and those who have been 'light linked' even in large groups, this they then take on themselves, if they are open to take on this assignment."

"Expect this to move out quickly when in place. Teach the facilitators to teach the next set of facilitators. Gather many as leaders as you will be guided to do. You no longer have to do it all."

"The holy door of secrecy is opening for advancement, and an initial financial cost can indeed be not the primary reason, but can be enticement to help with human expenses. Are you willing to serve in this position?"

"Of course", I reply, ready to serve.

OOO-LON: "Good then. Be now ready to begin. You are in agreement and open to serve whoever is drawn to extend themselves into the new paradigm and the new Keys."

"So then this session is at a close and we will be in contact so expect a City return as well as through your light corridor."

And as he said this he stood up, bowed, smiled, and we left this place of progress back on the trolley and through Gate Entrance into whatever steps are next.

I thank God and my teacher guides who move many forward into the City of Light demonstration.

So Light It Be.

On The Road Again

EMBASSY VISIT, December 1, 2009

The Gate of Entrance again appears as I enter into the vision unprepared for what to expect. The smile of La-Luke reminds me that this will be a special time and that we are headed for the Embassy. The wheel-less trolley pulls up as we exit the Park of Relaxation.

Entering this magnificent building filled with entities from all over the universe is a sight in itself to behold. Passing the head table with the five VIPs I bow and I take my usual place.

OOO-LON: "You have returned with questions on behalf of your planet?" I hear a familiar voice request.

GENII: "Yes. Well, sort of", I reply hesitantly. "I have been told that I will begin to see this City imprint. Is this correct?"

OOO-LON: "As said. This form of energy patterns is being fortified to be of service to you as others begin to sense there is something of evidence to their senses deeper than they may know. This, then, you will be able to verify as time releases its connection and the projected Major Shift takes hold. The days ahead will be exciting, yet in an unbalanced state as you are now experiencing."

GENII: "And what is my job in all this?"

OOO-LON: "The declaration of such an event of this magnitude will take you on trips of explanation. Ready all your data and be alert to new additions. Set your house in order, as you will have little time other than the City preparations. Take each day and utilize the home in production and preparation. Watch what new areas you are invited to enter and be selective."

" Rest is important, as your inner senses are enhanced to a high pitch and your senses become a constant announcement companion. The year coming soon will hold the Declaration of what is now being verified as sacred, holy, long since referred to as the Coming of Heaven on Earth, for it is so. So then are there any more questions for this session?"

GENII: "I am just so filled with love and gratitude for the information and the encouragement to continue so I may serve in the highest truth and honor. It is hard for me to express my feelings. Thank you."

OOO-LON: "All at this moment being said, go in peace and love and spread those feelings to all you contact. We honor your position and service."

With that, a feeling of dramatic love came from the faintly seen audience and we left, as I find myself back in Sedona with a deep knowing that indeed I am privileged to be a part of hearing and being part of the bigger unseen yet picture.

So Light It Be!

P.S. (more information) "The Genii is now in the light corridor as the City beams its frequencies into your world. These frequencies will make the Impression Imprint as you move forward...So Light It Be."

The Planeteers

CITY EMBASSY OF PEACE, December 23, 2009

The gate looked sparkly with lights beaming up to the heavens. I, in a holiday mood, met with my guide La-Luke. He has been such a gentle, loving support all these times. He looked a bit like Santa as his light gray beard took on the shine of the lights.

As he was dressed in white robes, he was indeed a vision to my eyes. I wondered what he would show me this visit. In any case, I am blessed to be able to take these inner vision visits and gather City information.

He took my hand and we almost ran thru the Park of Relaxation as he hustled me past the now parting willow trees what seemed to know we were on the way, and in here they probably did!

"Where to?" I gasped. As the trolley appeared I knew we were on the way to the City Embassy, a place of information and guidance from cosmic entities. Groovy. The wheel-less trolley whisked us to the doorway and we entered into this sanctuary of peace and advancement.

OOO-LON was also all decked out in white robes that reflected his inner love and respect for any guests who might enter. The almost unseen audience in the semi-light behind the CEO's at the front table sent forth a hum tone hat resonated through my body temple. We crossed to my seat and I felt I had just joined the upper crust of higher beings who were really unknown to me.

OOO-LON spoke: "Again during your earth festivities time, your wish was to come again and, thus, here you are. We are pleased to serve you. What may be your pleasure from us?"

GENII: "I know not what to ask. Well, maybe. I would like to know more about those who are part of this vast audience. Who are they, where do they came from and why?"

OOO-LON took a seat with those at his table. They all looked human but I sensed otherwise.

OOO-LON: "We who serve you are contained in a Cosmic Community where war or harm cannot be perpetrated by anyone as IT JUST DOES NOT EXIST. The universe is a plentiful place of entities who have developed through what you would call centuries beyond. This not behind. Beyond is the "before you" that we speak of here; 'future', if you will, in your language."

"They are referred to as 'Planeteers' who inhabit different planets, mostly unknown to you earth people, as your intelligence level has yet to make the leap except through your motion pictures and that shows only, for the most part, havoc and destruction."

"These Planeteers are not this. They are builders of Empires set in light frequencies that you would refer to as stars. Your development seekers call them dust particles, minerals, etc. This has been taught the target for eons of time yet unremembered by humans who struggle to maintain some kind of mechanical entry to bring forth the answers."

"Even the moon (so called) has levels of dimensions never before seen but maintains the outer facade to your astronauts' evaluations. Sky travel is limited only to now and then time slots as contact is sought with something other than earth. What is not understood or, for the most part, accepted by many is that contact was made eons ago and has been the primary source in fulfilling this current project that's aimed itself as a masterpiece of deliberate intention set in place to cure what has ailed this planet for far too long, and still continues in its light and darkness interlude under the guise of peace. This will not continue!"

"Dear one, you stand knowing better, due to years of interceptive work you were led into by the Dr. Bill. He was and is a prime leader to what you would call 'spilling the beans ' of this Divine Healing Demonstration. Does any of this make sense to you?"

GENII: "Oh, yes. Many years ago when my husband was channeling I asked if I could see the City before it is humanly seen. The answer was yes. It took a few years but I am astounded at what I have been prized to see and enjoy. Space ships and Extraterrestrials have always felt like friends and teachers to me. Even now as I write this, I feel such a surge of love and the tears flow easily. Why is this that I feel like I am just a visitor on earth?"

OOO-LON: "For this is so, as Lyra is your home base. Even though it seems many light years away it is in your heart as 'home.' It is one of those stars we spoke of earlier. The dimension you live in now is different because you are in human form, but another dimension exists within your light body that says what you have just asked. This information would take much time to explain, but soon you shall know the whole picture."

"Speak with Hermes and venture back here as questions equal answers and you are open to receive."

As this was spoken I knew the visit was over. My guide tapped me on the shoulder and we bowed as we headed out the door onto the trolley and back to the gate. My classroom is earth and my future unknown, but what the heck, look what I am finding out. Amazing! Thanks, God! **So Light It Be.**

Upward and Onward

EMBASSY VISIT, January 8, 2010

A new year invites me to request a trip back into the City of Light. Request Granted! With my energy fields in place and mentally aware and vision positioned, I peruse the visual Gate Entrance, five stories high, with my personal invite to return to the Embassy of Peace.

Once more my constant City guide appeared, gray white beard and all, in the image of La-Luke with a smile that made me think of Santa Claus in robes. The ooh's and ahh's of the people are loudly heard as they admire in amazement this holy place of light and healing.

I wondered: What if no healing of any kind was needed? Would there be a healing city needed? By the time this thought had had its way, I found us once again on the wheel-less trolley feeling a bit like Oz's Dorothy when she remarked, "Things come and go so fast here."

Maybe I am Dorothy on my way to meet the wizards, which certainly is what is inside the Embassy of Cosmic Information of universal travelers to this planet. It is no wonder I can get "spacey" on a daily basis at home with all this advanced far-out information I am privy to.

Head leader OOO-LON was standing as I now faced him from my conversation chair for what looked like a one-to-one conversation. The only sounds I heard were breathing sounds from the faintly-observed entities in the background that filled this huge place. I honored them and sat down. OOO-LON did likewise and he spoke the following:

OOO-LON: "We welcome you back to our City domain. How may we serve you?"

GENII: "For us on planet earth, changes are beginning in full force with weather, violence and people going crazy trying to figure out what is going on, much less handle it on a day-to-day basis. We salute this new year of 2010 even with the unstable conditions and conflicting minds looking for peace and stability. What can be said of these changes and the interest in 2012 ahead?"

OOO-LON: "It is observed that all you are reporting has validity and the predictions of a calmer peaceful world is still on the Books of Life fulfillment. Correct prophecies of such, an interpretation of ageless prophets who lovingly predicted this has set the course not only for themselves but also for cosmic entities who, though distant in the heavens, are nevertheless very important to the cleansing of this planet. What you do here has far reaching effects, and they are determined to support the efforts here, and have and continue to do so even today."

"Many on your planet think you are the only planet with intelligent life. Nonsense! Your planet is just a baby in the scheme of a cosmic community. What have your planet people done with what God has given you as a gift? Certainly drastic changes must be implemented for this planet to survive, or what would you have to walk on? Pay attention here! When a wound needs healing, do you not apply an antiseptic?"

"So the shake-up or shift is in process, not unlike a dog shaking off excess water from his fur. All this you are aware of, but it sets the scene for others to be in agreement with themselves by being aware. This may set the scene but not perhaps give you much comfort at the moment, but you can count on being able to handle it when you are aware what is coming into view as the healing edifice called the Holy City of Light."

"There will be planetary peace, and those of minds that would oppose this idea will leave by their own hands, as there are no victims, only creators, and all are creators."

"The dateline of 2012 leaves little time of completion, and all this turmoil will continue if left to its own devices. The Cosmic International Community united in its efforts of cleansing are gathered here in this domain of Light as we lovingly solve the problems the earth people give themselves. Like they have nothing else to do? Please! We make room for the new edifice you sit in at this moment."

(There was a hum in the auditorium behind him.) "This has been all preplanned, and even your part was included as a representative of what has been given you as a legacy left from your beloved husband, Dr. Bill."

"This God-man had many previously-impacted lives of service, and you know of his Hermes teachings. His background was vast with service and devotion, little of which he knew in this current life. When he departed this life he learned of this and is preparing his part in the City demonstration forthcoming. His preparation with the beginning City plans has given way to the extension that has been given to you to perpetuate further into the demonstration forthcoming. As said before, this City has been imprinted in your DNA and cannot be removed as it transmits the meaning you are to give forth."

"Now then, the Dr. Bill exits and you stand in for him and millions of others, as you hold court with what has been left you to serve and announce with . . . a legacy to be sure. And now what do you do with it?"

"Daily you feel your body in some kind of strangeness due to the mental change taking place that is unsettling but still part of your physical human form and must be, to report even if this is a bit shaky at the present moment. It too will pass away, finding your self stronger."

"Earthy support of friends and family who understand the place in which you find yourself can be helpful and supportive, as they understand that this is not an earthly so-called old age process. Quite the contrary, Elevation of Light is the title given from us."

"It is noticed that some of the earthly interests have little or no interest anymore, that you have your head in the clouds. Imagine that! But what is taking its place? Far out interests? Of course. Like Dorothy of Oz, you are going home while still on earth. Are you not learning Jedi ways?" (I nodded yes). "Your planet programming is that people forget, and you are hearing more and more of this, which includes you, on occasion."

"What is happening, Dear One, is that you are being brought into the 'Now' between the past and the future. A really nice place to be; no worries, no concerns, just being, even when the mind wants to keep the past from leaving. Persevere unto the end, for it will serve you well. As you say, not a problem!"

"You wonder how and where you will travel for announcing (with a companion of support.) We smile (and he did) as all is in process. Your electronic invention called computer internet (kindergarten style, though it may be at this point), has the opening to millions in one fell swoop. The contents of video and voice impacts the many, as what is being done now with the Charles at the helm sweeping up names and address of people who have more names and addresses et cetera is in progress. Is this not an avenue of progress?"

"The follow-up is in person. Would not people want to meet the real Genii? Of course! And as this year moves forward, expect the unexpected to appear as if by angels. Keep going. Dorothy's Emerald City of Light is right around the corner. So then, Lady of Light, what say you?"

GENII: (Trying to get a voice sound after all this) "Being in this place with all of you and hearing what has been said I am kind of speechless, but I recognize all is correct and right on schedule. I accept my place in what I can accomplish and will, to the best of my ability. Any extra energy and guidance will be appreciated."

OOO-LON: "Indeed. It would be wise to write out your questions for future visits to fill in the blanks, so to speak, and for now we excuse you to return back to your Sedona home where even today the energy fields are very active as you can feel and attempt to stay balanced. Quite a job, isn't it?"

And with that we stood and headed for the entrance. This was quite a process. And in a blink of an eye I was back home with my puppy who wants to play.

So Light It Be.

Going the Distance

EMBASSY VISIT, February 4, 2010

I entered into a quiet meditative state of consciousness. I also entered into the familiar south Gate of the City of Light, which shone bright and as clear as a crystal; a magnificent place to be sure. A rush of energy swirled around me and I knew that my Guide La-Luke had arrived. Did he ever! He grabbed my hand and whizzed me thru my favorite park with no stops on massage benches, and almost immediately I was ushered into the City Embassy of Peace Headquarters. What, no trolley ride? Things move fast here!

Immediately as we entered the Embassy all seems to be urgent. Maybe it was due to the constant light power surges I have been experiencing lately that has been said is a lifting of my light body frequencies. Okay, whatever.

The main leaders were in attendance, but there was also a new Entity there that stood up when they did, and I was moved to also stand in front of them. The energy level went up ... wow! This entity was almost transparent "it" was so light, or something.

OOO-LON welcomed me and said that this comrade was from a Cosmic Community far distant. Wow, this is getting interesting, and I don't even have to have a passport into space because they come here. Imagine that!

OOO-LON said: "He speaks not your language but that I would speak, for he brings a message of good tidings."

And with this, the frequencies around this Entity began to shift. Even his robe took on an unusual aura of soft color changes.

I thought, "This is beginning to be some kind of experience. Beginning? Maybe I am getting a cosmic consciousness?"

OOO-LON smiled as he read my thoughts. "Indeed", was his reply!

OOO-LON (speaking for the Entity): "I come from a place of far off distance many areas from this planet. I come to tell you, as a speaker of this place of healing, that destiny has arrived." (Here I got emotional with real tears).

"We are diminishing distance to bring forth this place yet unseen but destined. Your place in the whole of this is well established within the Community of Cosmic Dwellers. You have noticed that you are in the physical what you have been told are Light Power Surges within your light body. Is this true?"

I nodded yes.

OOO-LON continued speaking for this entity. They were sure connected, and even OOO-LON looked bit brighter. "You are being raised into an altered state of being and your connection to the Cosmic Community is well known."

GENII: "Who me?"

Through OOO-LON: "This is not to frighten you; in fact, it would be called, in your vernacular, a blessing. From this point forward, you can expect to enter into one of the cosmic-type interests as a Linking Consultant connecting of suffering people who would be welcomed into the City of Light Healing. Distance has collapsed and the City beckons the Genii to return for cosmic commands of events to take place on your planet, and you will be advised."

My feeling was agreeable but strange with all this, which could be overpowering if I permitted it to be. OOO-LON picked up my thoughts. A calmness fell over me that was quite pleasant, and I felt that I could go the distance somehow. To imagine that I have been presented with a Universal Community looking to have me do something is a long way from a stuttering high school dropout in Chicago, Illinois. I tool a deep breath as OOO-LON continued his friend's words.

Through OOO-LON: "The way of light has targeted areas of clean-up that are set in motion, and it has already begun. Consciousness is to be raised in many ways."

"It is important that you return here for guidance and introduction to yet more Entities of various cosmic communities not yet known." I was beginning to feel like an astronaut at ground level.

OOO-LON: "This is the message. 'Be aware. Be a person of courage, truth and honor. What you have been given indeed is factual evidence of the coming. Many will hear what others do not, due to its unusual strangeness, but necessary nevertheless.'"

With that, the Cosmic Entity sat down and OOO-LON nodded to me and asked if I knew what was taking place.

I did have a question. "I have recently met a man, Stephen Every, who I took through advanced teachings, that said seriously he feels he is a Space Ship Commander. What is to be known of this?"

OOO-LON: "Could this be so? Of course. This man has been led to you to learn of future City work he will do due to his training in advanced technology beyond this planet. Remember, you are excelling into the World of Universal contacts and anything is possible, even meeting a Space Vehicle Commander. Have we now taken your question to the world of answers?"

GENII: "Yes, way beyond what I could have ever imagined way back when this all started with Dr. Bill. Thank you. And learning of the Power Surges gives me an indication of elevation and a bit of sense in what I hear."

OOO-LON nodded as we left this cosmic chamber of light. And so I will go the distance, even if there is no distance to go. Imagine that!

Then the scene disappeared and I was back in Sedona looking at the sky with new eyes as I try to comprehend all this. It really is getting off the charts, unless they are heavenly charts that will guide our earth's course, and surely they are.

So Light It Be.

Community of Cosmic Dwellers

EMBASSY VISIT March 5, 2010. EXTRA TERRESTAL INTRODUCTION!

The Gate of Entrance structure loomed large and beautiful as I tapped into my screen of vision. It is seen as an evening with stars shinning in the heavens like crystal shards, but my real interest is to enter the Embassy and see what is up there. This is my 21st visit there and now being summoned sounds very exciting.

My guide, La-Luke, hustled me into the City Park and then onto the waiting trolley that whisked us to the Embassy of Peace in quick order. He said I was expected. There seemed to be some movement as we entered and headed for the now familiar head table and OOO-LON, the main speaker so far.

He stood alone and welcomed us with: "Welcome back to the Stellar Community of Space Dwellers here to serve." The amphitheatre-type building began to hum. I looked around past him into what had been seen faintly before, and as it began to get a bit lighter I could see hundreds of entities unfamiliar to me.

I tried to make out their appearances but I was only able see them faintly. However, I just knew they were special because I could feel the love that was sent to me from row after row after row. I could have floated away on that energy. Now this is real, total love and I am the recipient. The knowingness made tears flow down my face. Imagine that!

We need to let people know there is nothing to fear from ETs. They are and have been helping us for God knows how long.

OOO-LON smiled as he announced, "These are community friends from cosmic universities who have long since banned together with each of their kind in a force field to bring forth the City of Light here and the salvation of your planet which needs to band with those I have just spoken of sitting here in unison."

With this I was speechless!

GENII: "I am so honored that I can hardly speak to be with such a vast intelligent audience, as I always have had an interest in space deities. We humans may see UFOs on occasion but this is something else. Wow!"

I am so excited I have to sit down in overwhelm.

OOO-LON: "As expected. As you are well aware, the universe is a hologram and each one here is one with the center creator as you call God, but there is more to this. Each one here is from spaces beyond spaces that are a part of the hologram with the intent of expanding the light lines connecting a force field of a universal power that brings your people peace, love and a healing facility never before seen on this planet. Does this make any sense to you?"

GENII: "Yes, we all are connected to the one center of a universal holographic center source, and being this, the cosmic community banded together with intelligence energy forces so they and we could bring into view the City of Light with healing technology of light probably not known here. Is this correct?"

OOO-LON: "There is much more advanced thinking, but this will do for the moment. Now then, I would have you meet a friend from the banded community of universal knowing, Sa-Daaa, who shares with you further."

From the shadowy background an entity came into view. I guess it is a he. He walked on two legs, had two arms, his wide hands had six fingers and his skin was a light orange color with tiny bumps all over it. His face was not scary but quite nice, with the head section being in sort of a triangle shape, no nose to speak of, black eyes like the night sky, and a small indentation of a smile. I just fell in love with him as he sent me such a groovy unusual feeling. Golly, a new far-out friend. Imagine that. God is so good to me.

OOO-LON spoke for him: "This is Sa-Daaa, and he wishes you to know that the work on the City has been completed and that his community declares that their part is over and supplied with the Sa-Daaa technology that has been inserted."

GENII: "What else am I to know?"

OOO-LON: "Prepare yourself and as many as possible because in the days ahead the energy fields will pick up and the sensory indications of the planet will change into one that is compatible with the City. All cosmic communities will now enter into the final stages of this centuries-old project with frequencies beyond what has been experienced before."

"Time, as has been said, is short term and the immediacy as spoken of will begin to be felt, but much more. Be aware of new instructions to come forth and move with them as guided. Now, then, is there anything else? The stability of the humans will alter the present conditions and be the way the planet itself will survive."

GENII: "Yes. Where does Sa-Daaa come from?"

OOO-LON: "Many eons of space away and from a small planet, but he is dedicated to see this one survive. It is called (but in a tonal language) Cervan-Delka; the tones and the sounds of the universe. This one is not on your sky maps but we will send you picture mental imprints periodically from him so you can enjoy his home place."

"Just be open to receive. All is well and in progress. So then know that indeed all is well and we shall be in touch to move you forward into your world of announcement."

I gratefully bowed as I felt the energy lift in the building, making me feel a bit weak as we moved outside. The air was fresh and the stars, as I looked up to them, seemed to wink back at me.

And so ends another visit to the Embassy of Peace.

So Light It Be!

Seeing the Unseen

CITY EMBASSY OF PEACE VISIT April 24, 2010

The five story entrance gate stands tall before me and I wondered if the City illumines the Sun or does the Sun illumine the City. It is pretty awesome anyway one looks at it. Many people are heading through the Gate portal as I see my guide approaching.

La-Luke has been my friend for eons of visits. Today he ushers me through the arch, through the park of relaxation and on to the familiar trolley that takes us to a mammoth building that gathers entities from various parts of the universe who have been, in their way, responsible in bringing forth this City of Light and Healing, the Embassy of Peace!

Head speaker OOO-LON stood up along with 4 others who hold court in front of this assembly, as I am assisted toward my usual chair. As he stands, a hum is heard behind him in the background. I feel very welcome indeed.

OOO-LON: "We welcome you back oh feminine of light, into the history being made for your planet and we speak to you for a few moments."

I nodded not knowing what to expect. He continued..." The emphasis of the City of Light is on its three- dimensional approach, and progress has been made. No longer can you have any doubts, for in their subtle areas, it will begin to be seen by you. Very faint at first, but the progress of its appearance, and with your mental/ physical endurance of late, the portals open for your inspection and light."

"Long since have you been aware of such a happening and now you can test your sanity for the light powered image you will see will testify what has been said for so long. Is this understood?"

I nodded and replied, "Is there something I should be doing to support what has just been said?

OOO-LON smiled. "Dear one you have the City embedded in your DNA, heart and mind and now, as the outer vision begins to appear slowly at first, just know that what you are seeing is accurate and enjoy the view."

"This will take time for you to get used to … the new vision outlines … but know that you are supported by all who sit in the assembly and on all levels. Stay with your heart attached and permit love to be your guide as you do now, in your world in preparation for the vision to appear, thus making more light in your world. Is this agreed?"

Surely he jests, I thought. Would I not want to see the greatest show this earth ever had? Then a smile from those in front told me they knew what I was thinking...duh!

"Of course" OOO-LON continues," It will be observed in bit parts. A bit here, a sight form there, which may surprise you as this will seem new, as you live your daily life through your integral guidance. You already see the cloud forms that tell you that they cover the space vehicles in the vicinity but people just see the clouds. Is all this clear?"

"Yes, I am fine. Oh ... I would love to have conversations with any space entity who would like to share with me."

OOO-LON: "We shall set that on the agenda and invite you to sit in. Be light, be the love that you are. Remember the High Court and your Adornment of Internal Love and all will be well with you!"

With that we all stood, bowed, and I turned to travel with my guide to the entrance, the trolley, the park and out the gate where at this time I find myself relaxing on my bed with all my desires fulfilled. Nice start for this day. What's next?

Thanks God … All is perfect .7: 23 am

P.S. As I looked out over the red rocks of Sedona from my bedroom window I could see white light like a rock aura. Wow!

So Light it be, for you and me.

Love, Genii

Speaking the Language of Space

EMBASSY OF PEACE HEADQUARTERS, June 19, 2010

Walking into the scene at the gate, I am in the company of my Guide La-Luke and what a neat Guide he is. I am blessed. My purpose is that I have requested as suggested, to meet and speak with an entity from Outer Space.

Moving through the Park onto the usual driverless trolley we arrive at the Embassy, and I find myself standing in front of the head table with OOO-LON and his usual co-partners (which have never spoken to me), and also this time, a new Entity stands with him.

He looks human-type but I felt this was some kind of maybe a covering, to put me at ease but that he really was an Entity from somewhere in space. He wore a long robe that glowed under his long white hair that hit the floor, and he had a short white beard as a matched set.

His face was pleasant. He had no nose to speak of, but big eyes that could melt the planet with love and his mouth was kind of off to one side. What I did feel from him was total love and I recognized that they have to get used to us too. We are the strange looking ones.

We are so used to seeing film entities that look more like us than what they really are (do). So I am getting sort of acclimatized I guess. OOO-LON also looks humanized a bit, but it seems that he is today's spokesperson for whatever.

OOO-LON: "And your mission today is?"

Genii: "It has been said that I was to come back and to meet an extraterrestrial and learn what I could understand from them."

OOO-LON: "Yes this is true and beside me is a friend from the ethers of space. He is a connected brother whose mission is to assist in bringing forth what you stand in now."

Genii: "We are used to seeming depictions of space entities but mostly in human design. So anything else is quite foreign."

OOO-LON: "This then is another meeting. Dressed in a robe of light you would understand, I introduce you to 'Meeeeeeeee Ka Laaaaaaaa' who speaks only space dialect. He uses a tone for a contact name so we have connection in not language, as you speak, but in tones of the universe. This is a whole other programming."

"We speak space so this is no problem for us. You have been taught the tones of love, connection and healing in your 4 Keys Atonement series so dear one, that is a beginning only but useful as you know. Questions of him?"

Genii: "Where are you from?"

Answer through OOO-LON: "My home is many light years away. If distance is an important level of understanding, I enter your light fields from a space place of harmony and advanced teaching. It would be sounded as 'TUR-A-KA' in your tonal language."

Note: As he was sounding the tone I began sinking farther into deeper meditation.

OOO-LON continuing for him: "I come from a home far beyond the earth tone. The City call was to me a call of space unsettlement, where interference for the good of this planet is needed, and we who inhabit the cosmic tonery answered the call. The un-sensing of love in most people here upsets the harmony of the universe and must be put to rest. My people only know the tones of what you call LOVE and this planet must conform, so balance is maintained in the Cosmic Communities."

Note: Just hearing this and being in his presence, I kept spacing out a bit . . . understandably so I guess. The frequencies were higher than mine and I could hardly write what was being said, much less in long hand. I needed some air.

OOO-LON "Speaking space has deep energy attached and is effecting you so, I think it would be best for this visit to resume at another time. I suggest that you take these space talks very easy ...as your energy field needs getting used to it, and this is part of what is taking place with your humanness now daily."

The entity nodded and I asked to be excused and it was lovingly agreed. With thanks and appreciation La Luke led me out to the door and took me to the Gate. I now find myself home, trying to write about speaking space and the power those frequencies give in feeling.

More questions to be asked soon.

So Light it be!

Somewhere Between Heaven and Earth Where Magic Never Ends

EMBASSY OF PEACE HEADQUARTERS, July 11, 2010

The vision begins with my guide and me already at the embassy. I had sensed that I was to return. Those in attendance included OOO-LON, and those at the head table with him, bid us welcome and motioned us to be seated. I felt that something important was to be discussed.

OOO-LON: "We in attendance bid you welcome. From the far reaches of outer space, the body of this assembly is created from those of the Cosmic Community previously spoken of. We have set forth in order the following....

1. That within the period of your time, the City of Light will make its appearance within the next year's end!

2. Those who have diligently produced this City and its healing techniques are on course to see it in performance.

3. The Genii has always been interested in the far off reigns of cosmic places in wondering who and what may be found there. The world as you know it is about to become one of those in the outer galaxies due to the City's dramatic event.

4. Much has been said of the lower consciousness of your people thus, the raising is necessary for the benefit of all who live in cultured lands of other dimensional latitudes of space.

5. Light knows that no darkness can continue to develop when it is pulsating from the creator and that includes everyone. It is the people in their confused ego states that are primary in producing what has taken place on your planet. This will be stopped through alteration of their confused mental from destruction to peaceful ways.

6. We are preparing to introduce you to your Cosmic Community neighbors who can share through an interrupter, to give you a larger picture of what has been put together for the benefit of mankind (such as it is).

7. The master teacher, one of several, of so long ago attempted to teach the true meaning of love as do many today. Now is the time to set the course with a deeper understanding of what and who are your universal family.

8. Your screened motion picture of Avatar gave you a sample of another world of those who lived and loved until man entered to destroy through greed.

Many such locations of stars and planets know only love and as the Genii knows as 'pure love!' and anything else is foreign to their thinking.

9. The time has arrived as the Genii has inherited this kind of love and sends it forth to those she knows. Love is the strongest vibration of healing for it encompasses the heart to heart, which is the vital organ and power center in the body. As has been said recently between the Genii and a close friend, "it is the 'pure love' that knows no boundaries which is far beyond what is normally known." Pure? Indeed!

So then, what questions do you propose?"

Genii: "What am I to know or ready myself for?"

OOO-LON: "More visits here. Be ready to meet any entity you are introduced to and be attentive to what they share. You are considered a 'unit' and will be unified with them."

Genii: "Will I be able to carry on a kind of normal life? I do have to get the City information to do whatever it is supposed to do."

OOO-LON " Yes, some things will seem different as you have a path like no other, that very few walk, and those who know of your path will support you and your findings as self united."

Genii: "Staying balanced is interesting."

OOO-LON: "It is knowing that the energy forces of two worlds holds your interests. Be easy with you. Anything else?"

Genii: "If I am meeting an entity from space what am I to be prepared for?"

OOO-LON; "Love and friendship, wisdom, and advanced knowledge simply put for your understanding."

Genii: "Thank you."

OOO-LON; "Go now and think on this with the suggestion that you re- see the Avatar movie and eliminate the darkness as much as possible and tune into the love of these people. It is similar to what you will find ahead."

And with this the scene ended and I am home at 7:21 am, amazed at the opportunities coming forth before me.

THANKS GOD!

Do You Speak Space?

July 27, 2009

INTRODUCTION TO COSMIC WAYS

In the early quiet of a summer Sedona morning I mentally permit to wait until I enter another dimension where I have been previously invited. In vision now I stand at the same gate as usual with a few people scattered here and there admiring this massive five-story entrance. It was here that I heard a voice say, "Behold, I bring you glad tidings of great joy". Whether it was on a loud speaker or just in my head I am not sure, but it did make one feel they were in the right place at the right time.

I move myself through the gate and into the park and onto a massage bench. What a great feeling to begin any tour. I opened my eyes from this deluxe moment to see this park was empty. (My people come and go quickly.) At this point my vision went totally blank; no picture, no sound, nothing for a few seconds.

Upon seeing again, there before me stood not one, not two, but three male robed entities. They smiled and nodded for me to rise and follow. I did, and as we passed through the very large willow trees, one went to the left and one to the right while the third took my arm and we went ahead. "Where now?" I wondered.

We walked only a short distance when before us was a building that was shaped like a flying saucer space vehicle. Now, some of the white buildings I have seen did have space vehicles like gold domes on them, but I'd bet this one couldn't fly. I wondered if we were going there. As I said this, I picked up an unusual energy buzz from the top of my head to the ground, and I swear I lifted an inch off. This was like Sci-Fi stuff, and I was getting excited!

We walked in through the misty shielded doorway, and by golly it did look something like a space interior like in the movies but all peaceful and no anxiety anywhere. It was really quite pleasant. Okay, now what? Coming through another entrance was another male that, when I looked at him his face changed a bit, kind of like what Wayne Dyer said, "Change the way you look at things, and the things you look at will change". (I'm not sure he meant it that way but . . . ?)

This one was really changing, one minute looking like a human sort and the next something else, not bad or gruesome just a flick, change. It was mesmerizing, but fun.

"Welcome", was the sounding word that seemed to float in the air like a melody. "You speak space?"

"Ah, what does that mean?" I said slowly.

"It is obvious that you do not, so we will speak in your tongue. Come and sit with me," he replied, and he led me into another so called 'pod', and he suggested I just call it a room. Whatever. He was dressed in a kind of uniform, with soft light blue fabric that ... oops, that is changing as well. Oh, my.

"You are interested in Jedi ways?"

"Yes", my answer came quickly."

"You wish no darkness of mind?"

"Yes," I replied.

"The measure of light and darkness of thinking makes for havoc on your planet. We are here to change that concept, not to control anyone. Quite the contrary."

"Excuse me. Who are you and am I having an illusionary moment?" He leaned back and smiled, or at least I think it was a smile.

"I am Taluna, Master of Illusionary Premonitions, and this building is so futuristic in your world. Some might not even see it or would feel it is a figment of the mind. This building exists for several reasons here in the City of Light . You have been to the Embassy of Light and have seen many entities in the large theater seated in the background. Is this so?"

GENII: "Yes," I say, trying not to look excited.

TALUNA: "Your wish is being granted as we take an advanced tour, and you will see what light projections can really accomplish within a short period of time. This City of Light is for advanced healing techniques, and little by little we have introduced new ways to use light in your laboratories to be found and used. As you know, it takes far too long to cure with the slow methods now being used. Now masters of these light healings make so called new break-throughs that they think they have invented, and they did, with a little help from unseen friends."

"Your movies and films depict anything from beyond this planet must be either untrue or out to make trouble, like in the Jedi movies, et cetera, except for a few where positive is the basis of the film. With us it is all light, and only love penetrates, for that is what light is."

GENII: "Is this why I am so interested in Jedi techniques and laws?"

TALUNA: "Precisely. You have seen the Jedi performances many times. Would you like to meet real Jedi masters and understand what they really represent?"

GENII: "Oh, yes," quickly came my reply.

TALUNA: "Then we shall have you return to this Jedi training center and you can be given instructions to heighten your human understanding of just what power is."

And with that he stood up, raised his hand over my head and I felt a love shiver from the top of my head to the ground, going straight through my body like I have never felt before.

GENII: "You mean there is really a process of Jedi-ing?" I stood up as he continued.

TALUNA: "Of course. Where do you think the movies got the idea in the first place? And are you not to speak about the City, which runs on this premise behind the scenes?"

GENII: "Well, I do have a Light Saber."

He laughed as he said, "Play toys. Come be in the Jedi world for a bit and see what helps make this healing city a City of Light and Healing."

With this he stepped out, and I was led to follow back to the gate where I was met by my original guide, La-Luke.

La-Luke looked at me and said, "Well, how was that?"

GENII: "Oh, guess what I get to learn? The Jedi ways!"

LA-LUKE: "I know. Congratulations," he replied, and promptly disappeared.

And I did too, back to Sedona to continue my day in my world, knowing it was going to be good because I am happy. Imagine that!

The Magic Advantages of Light

EMBASSY VISIT, August 8, 2010

Thoughts of The Embassy of Peace bring forth the future, and as I enter into this realm in thought and vision, delight and honor fills my heart. The five-story gate complex (How many times have I been here now?) seems to welcome me and others who are all excited to enter. A tap on my shoulder awakens my amusement of what I see, as my guide La-Luke readies me for the dash to the trolley that takes us to the Universal Embassy of Light and Peace.

Arriving at The Embassy building, we are ushered into the Sanctuary of Light. Beings from all over the universe gather here together in preparation to move all forward in the expectancy of The City demonstration. What a privilege to be here. Oh My! … Yes!

Head Master OOO-LON and his front table companions rise to the occasion as we enter and are seated nearby in a seat of visiting honor. I have been here so many times that I feel at home in the awesome football stadium kind of building. So somewhere in time, once more I get the privilege of conversations with the highest beings one could meet. In some ways this is just pure fun and powerful in its reality. And the conversation begins …

OOO-LON: "Welcome Light Lady to the meeting of 'Beings from parallel universes' and the universe of wisdom and knowledge par none. What may we entice you to say?"

Genii: "First permit me to thank you all for your love, wisdom, and encouragement to continue with The City announcements. It is always a deep honor to be in your presence of such vast wisdom. I have a few questions … one from City Light Renee Trenda who is announcing the City wherever she can, even to the presidents for contact with me."

OOO-LON: "This is good and fruitful, continue … "

Genii: "She asks, "Is there some genetic factor in our bodies that would let us connect with these Universal Uniphase Power Capsules, so that we may emit more Light? Are we in any way connected to the UPPCs?"

OOO-LON: "Actually No. Your power centers are designed to hold just so much amperage and the packaged UPPC's would be too strong to manage. You just would not be anymore. However, the spin-off from the capsules does emit Light, and since you are this, you would feel the essence of them. With the City there is no way you would not be subject to the frequency dwelling in the City itself."

Genii: "Her second question ... 'Would the UPPC's be a Free Energy device for homes and businesses to replace fossil fuel?'"

OOO-LON: "To a certain extent. As The City enters into the human equation of demonstration, it will appear that there is more here that can be used in other areas of support as she has questioned."

"Remember this is the first City! There are imprints in the Ethers of sameness, that will appear and the Light is to be emitted from them, as has been said to you."

"This planet of humans will glow in the heavens like another moon that was hand-placed by God. The change-over on your planet will have that much frequency. It is known by us that words are just words until the seeing is observed. But, you can mark these words of offering ... that this indeed is so! For this place of Earth, much energy frequencies must be amplified and will be, due to the High Towers process of catching and relaying the UPPC's as they will into each City in the Ethers, thus lightening up many miles around also."

"What you have entered here with the first City, is the attention-getter! And this will fascinate more advanced ideas to come forth in balancing out the planet's darker spots, while also bringing forth more scientific areas to hone in on, which will make the world take another look at itself with what is called 'New Eyes.' Science and spirit will walk hand-in-hand for progress is essential, and will not be by-passed. This is a promise."

"Many entities have been instrumental, and instruments of peace are in this House of Peace Headquarters that you attend at this moment. These are minds so far beyond the Earth that the good that is about to change people's thinking, through new frequencies that are even now bombarding your planet, is beyond normal human thinking."

"Those who work in various areas such as Earth plants and greenery, will rejoice in the way the plants respond to normal light emanating from any of the future Cities of Light, and all in-between as nothing is left out. What needs to be cleaned out, will be. What needs to be replenished, will be!"

"Take note: Hundreds upon hundreds of humans are leaving in various ways and are supporting the cleansing from another level. Even those with darkened minds now see the Light from a different perspective. Those who have suffered in the wars will find comfort and healing and release of mental wounds. This too is part of the Light Healing. Nothing is left out ... nothing! And as said, the wars will have no more attraction to exist!"

Genii: "Is there an update on the City appearance?"

OOO-LON: "As said, as the minds concentrate on 2012 … leading up to that date makes the City a silent appearance, and people with an average sense will sense something is going to happen. The dark minds will feel that it is some kind of disaster. The light minds will feel the love to such an extent that even without knowing it, they will assist the energy to bring it forward."

"Those who respond have the lead in, and their leadership of Light will assist others to spread the word in welcome of what is to be seen. The days come and go quickly now. The emphasis is on contact and spreading the message to those who will hear and respond within themselves. There is yet time for The Genii and other City Lights to spread the word, but not much. So then, can we be of more help?"

Genii: "Thank you all, and as I am invited, I will return."

OOO-LON: "Do that, for your advancement beyond the Earth as much is yet to be discovered and shared. For this point, continue to serve as people recognize that what you say is truth-connected. Rest and play to keep yourself in good condition. We bid you the Light of the eternal day!"

And with this, I find myself at home in Sedona and ready to ride off to Disneyland for a well-earned few days vacation, and the green bench on Main St. chatting with Walt Disney … Imagine that!

So Light it be!

World Changes Ready or Not!

EMBASSY VISIT, August 21, 2010

The gate that I normally enter is awesome to behold and I move with others excitedly and optimistically through this horseshoe entrance with my City Guide La-Luke running us to the trolley, and heading to the Embassy of Peace.

How many times have I been here now? 30-40-50? No matter, each time is important and I am honored to be ushered into the sanctuary before me. Within a few minutes, we were standing before this High Tribunal of Space Entities from various parts of the universe. The energy of love and wisdom penetrates my system.

OOO-LON: "I trust that you had good experiences since we last entered into conversation of unknown commodities?"

GENII: "I do my best to stay balanced in these two worlds. It is not always easy."

OOO-LON: "As stated, this will pass as you again are to move forward into the east dawn land. You have questions?"

GENII: "I am told a sound or sounds from the universe will announce The City appearance to be delivered."

OOO-LON: "Yes."

GENII: "What sounds am I listening for?"

OOO-LON "You have been carrying a static type sound in your head ever since The City was introduced to you many years ago. Is this correct?"

GENII: "Yes, both Dr. Bill and I noticed it about the same time and it has been on constantly ever since, sometimes higher than other times, but I ignore it most of the time."

OOO-LON: "You are aware that what you hear is your Light System like an electrical ensemble. You are aware of this also?"

GENII: "Yes, Long since."

OOO-LON: "This denotes that your system has been tuned in for some time now. The sound from the universe will become obvious. Again it is advised to re-watch the movie 'Contact' and to pick up the subtleties unsaid. The catch phrases are signal points for you to be aware."

"We are aware that you are a novice in this aeronautics area, but have no concerns. It will be known. Your mental and physical accoutrements will tone you in."

GENII: "OK. I am open to what is expected of me to be experienced. I am about to travel to the Chicago area to meet someone new. What can be said of this as guidance as to what I am to take with me and do actually?" (Hum was registered in the background).

OOO-LON: "Any location trip you take, always take The City material for people will be deliberately put on your path. You are to serve as an advancement spokesperson of the coming important events and those who can hear, will hear."

"We attempt to advise you of what is possible for the City energy coming into your dimension is in full force, making upheaval something traumatic. Your planet people will react in many unusual ways and some not to the liking of most. Who wants to be uncomfortable? It is in the 'un' that the comfort births."

"The massive energy structure makes waves of its forthcoming, and you see people not able to withstand these frequencies, and go what you would call 'crazy.' The destructiveness in these events are an introduction of massive changes and most are unaware and could not understand the frequencies they themselves are causing."

"You have had centuries upon centuries of mental and physical warfare, and to change all that to a peaceful existence is a massive experience in itself. You have no idea of that which has gone on before to bring this to a demonstration conclusion and will continue as such."

"At this point, it is incomplete. Try as we may and do, this planet of Earth people resist change in any shape or form, and in doing so, that very resistance brings them forth more harm than good."

"It has been repeated over and over that you are 'source energy.' Do your people know what that means when they run amuck, doing dangerous things and then wonder why that happened? We think not."

"You are what is called in your dimension, God! But no, who can declare that? Would one be blasted down or hung on a cross? Stupidity runs amuck and to bring sanity into your planet takes all of those you see here in this sanctuary and more besides. We are what you are, in different costumes but the same never-the-less. Imagine That!"

"You direct your energy to do what you want like sending your light through your 'light saber' like a Jedi Master would, but for good of the whole, with love, not hate and malice and blame and all the dark forces data you are aware of.

People bring on their own demise, planet changes etc. It cannot be otherwise! You people do it all. Congratulations! Understand? You understand?"

GENII: "OH Yes! ... Very well!"

OOO-LON: "Then you are well aware of what is taking place and the absolute need of the City demonstration to materialize into form. Will this shake up various locations, be it mentally and physically? ... Of course! How else can the new be born ... and be a clean clear planet be ready to intertwine with others in the universe? Something of major proportions must take place ... and it will ... and it is!"

"It has been said that this year of 2010 would be seen as tumultuous and has this not been the case? Things that never happened ever before are making newspaper headlines. Hello world. Pay attention here lest you miss the real reason. Those who have done wrong will learn of a better side of themselves through their own beliefs."

"Again, you are this ... God incarnate, source energy, The I AM ... Imagine that!"

"Ahhh! Wait ... pay attention here ... don't by-step this for it is not ego on a rampage, but truth in the heart with such deep love attached. It has been said by a friend that, "It is either love or it isn't." What has been in the energy fields is not love in the truest sense ... but mark these words, it will be ... it will be!" (Again a hum echoed in the background).

GENII: "What can I do? What are my instructions?"

OOO-LON: "Stay in balance as much as possible. We understand that with your work, to stay grounded is almost impossible, and we support as we can. Listen for indications of the tone of the City. Be open to share and in doing so, change people's vibrations and attachments of fear, for as said 'God can do anything and we add ... will!"

"Be easy with your system. Rest and continue to love deeply everyone you meet, for your love and honor are very strong. Delete any negativity of words and actions from others. They have no place with your mission for love and light is far more dependable, and you have these qualities beyond most."

GENII: "Thank you. I will fulfill my mission as best I am guided."

OOO-LON: "You are closer to the demonstration than ever before. Be easy with you as your automatic electronic system is in a massive change. Enjoy what you have demonstrated. Take your love trips and spread the word and expect it to become more intense as the word passes and the energy lifts the people to understand what is taking place. They will find you. Be open and giving of these words."

"So then, return again and we shall see what next steps are to be taken. You are doing very well. Stay only in the God love for that is what heals and see the world you live in become a peaceful situation even during the change-over."

Then, I turned and my guide La-Luke led me to the trolley. I hugged him. No words were needed or even spoken after that. And now I find myself home ready to type this all up from my hand-written sights and sounds.

Blessed am I? You bet!

SO LIGHT WE ALL ARE.

Cosmic Communities and Such

EMBASSY VISIT, September 7, 2010

Arriving at the gate entrance, many people were seen excited to also enter. Looking around for my City Guide La-Luke, I felt him grab my hand and like the parting of the seas, he rushed me through the crowd to the wheel-less trolley and in a flash we were in the Embassy of Peace. We were standing in front of the four entities in robes, with OOO-LON standing in a greeting position. Entering into this building is always exciting for the possibilities of such vast learning are always available.

The welcome mat was out. With OOO-LON's hand extended, I am very comfortable. What a dear soul he is ... I've never found anything other. And if all E.T.'s are like this, there is nothing to worry about; actually quite the contrary. It is a vast community that spreads across the heavens of which we are a part ... thank goodness.

OOO-LON: "Welcome Oh Lady of Light who walks the earth with great news of the coming attraction. How may we serve you?"

Genii: "I am so happy to be back at this time. I do have some questions."

OOO-LON: "Serve us, so we can serve you."

Genii: "Close friends are seeking to build local communities before the City arrives. What can be said of the Universal Cosmic Communities that would be of support with advanced Cosmic guidance to be incorporated into what would be best for the Earth dwellers?"

(There was a big sigh heard from the almost invisible audience of Extra Intelligence behind these leaders.)

OOO-LON: "Yes...the time has arrived that this question is not out of order. People banding together make progress as long as 'LOVE' is the leader and we find patches of it even through this changeover your planet is experiencing. On one place we see man killing man and on the opposite we see man loving man. Which is best?"

"Those of us who are from far off Space Places with unknown names do not fight like what is presented in the moving pictures such as the Star Wars series. It just is not encouraged, nor even thought of. We are not programmed as such. This is barbaric as ignorance tries to become Light by killing off what it would be. Strange thinking!"

"From one Star Community to another peace reigns supreme. It is recognized again that only the frequency of 'LOVE' equals the power. Did not the Jedi master Yoda recommend LOVE to be the answer? Indeed, to advance and visit one Star Cluster to another, war is not even a slight consideration much less conquest or over-taking another. It just does not happen."

"Do you not call the upper level thinking Heaven? Now we.... bring you Heaven on Earth!"

"So then, where is the LOVE in building a Cosmic Community on the Earth plane? It is much needed and in line to gather those who respond to love (there is a feeling that one is of that persuasion.) You say you want peace ... you say you want love ... you say you want oneness. What are the people demonstrating? Your planet is a Community but unlike the Cosmic Sense it is divided into pieces and parts as each person may not honor another."

"You all call yourselves the United States. Excuse us but what is united here? Where are the means of compassion in the division of what we see?"

"Those in your close realm of friends seek to hold a piece of ground here and there as a Light Center of LOVE that can attract others to also be light carriers. A community can indeed do this when under the banner LOVE. Dear ones THIS IS COSMIC ADVANCEMENT!"

"So then to have guidance from this vast Cosmic Community (as sits behind us in this building of light), one must begin with LOVE. When a few are gathered in God's love, it then has drawing power to bring forth anything that is needed to secure land etc. for the desired community contact."

"Open with advanced LOVE and permit God to fill in the connections with the same frequencies of LOVE. From this, come the divine ideas and advanced technology as used in the City. All this is cosmic heart light center equivalent. Have we given you any ideas of starting?"

Genii: "Yes, love is all that opens the doors of any community."

OOO-LON: "Yes this is true ... simply explained in the Energy Fields of Attraction. Any more questions?"

Genii: "Yes. In another area, my friend Renee Trenda and I have just come back from a trip to the President Carter Center to deliver the gift of the re-creation of a miniature marionette to him, and the manuscript of the City of light. What are the next steps?"

OOO-LON: "Patience in waiting for a response will pay off as you say. The President will become an interested reader. Wait upon the Lord, so to speak."

Genii: "Anything else?"

OOO-LON: "Just remember to LOVE and all will be well and the advanced City reports of progress will become nearer than your breath."

"Begin your 'Cosmic Community Center' and see what is drawn in. Use the Advanced Achievement Academy site. Go and light the path before you all. Gather, connect, process data, and thus fulfill prophecies long since declared."

"God lights the path before you all. We now release you to re-enter your home and begin your day with recording this report and entrance into the new City of Light Book with the Charles understanding the method of entrance for printing. You must have printed copies on hand to help support the Light Center of God thus communicating with many communities."

With this, he bowed as a hum ran through the background audience and I feel such love and not of earth-kind but so much deeper. We left the Embassy and I find myself home with my puppy looking for a hug... Hey...it's all about LOVE, Right?

Thanks God, this was God Good!

So Light it be...

And It Came Upon A Midnight Clear!

EMBASSY VISIT, October 5, 2010

In the expectation of going to a Mike Dooley seminar and meeting of the universe, I happily find myself at the familiar gate towers along with many others. La-Luke arrived and we set off to the Embassy which I now feel so comfortable in, filled with universal entity friends of love and light. The usual trolley takes us to the Embassy door and we sense that we are anticipated by those inside … and we are.

The leaders at the table greet us just with their vibrations as OOO-LON extends his hand which is almost non-existent to me, but I can feel the energy putting me at ease and in serenity.

OOO-LON: "Once more we meet and exchange ideas to further your role of expectancy. Where shall we begin?"

Genii: "Anticipating that an up-dated City manuscript is almost ready to be printed, I wondered if there was anything more to be included from the Embassy and those here present."

OOO-LON: "The prospect that this issue brings people's interests closer to understanding of the messages given, we have a few words [or designs as we call them] to be inserted from our combined thoughts of we who know of the completion and vibration and entrance of this City and it's healing properties. Thus, you may say........

"Upon the setting of a sun, and during the quiet of a night, there will be set on your earth surface for sun-up visual-made-seeing, a God-made invention of healing through many technologies that have not ever before been known."

"No one has to fly into outer space or land on another planet to see if life really exists, or if you are the only planet with life on it. Forgive me, but this is a ridiculous belief that you are the only place of honor and we smile with anticipation of your knowing the real truth, and as soon as we come to you."

"So save some mental spaces to know and recognize all that has been foretold, now appears, and your world will never be the same again as a massive change is not only needed but desired by masses of earth people."

"The time has arrived for this Change of Consciousness and we believe that this demonstration will do just that! Centuries upon centuries it has taken to build, for a 3-dimensional seeing and using. Divine intervention now fulfills that prophesy of a Master long since."

"Too many separate themselves from the original creator of all. So then now, pay attention to what was, and to what is now words of instruction from universal beings [all in the unseen] to make this prophesy come to light."

"So then dear one, Genii of the Light Lamp with vibrations beyond the normal, take these words, for they are vibrations of truth and with them set into place 'The COMING' for it is indeed and people will cry 'halleluiah!' Time is non-assistant at this point but in your vernacular it is important."

"So let it be known that we Universal Beings of Community Light, now declare this to be so. Now the clock ticks faster. . .

So light it be!"

With this then, I sense that all those in the auditorium that I could only see faintly, sounded the universal tone of AH that I share in the Sacred Teaching on Four Keys to Light.

It almost blew me over and then the lights in this place went on and I could see hundreds up hundreds all standing in various colors and designs. I am speechless ... so much so that La-Luke held me and we exited ... and I now find myself home at the bark of my pup 'Light'. I am blessed.

A Closing Embassy of Peace Message

Received July 27, 2010

OOO-LON: "Permit it to be known to anyone reading this message, that the Embassy of Peace Genii visits have not concluded, however the contents of the previous visits contained within these pages are enough to stir the imagination into the credibility of the dramatic presentation coming on the earth stage, are correct in the information given."

"Some will say in reading this, 'I will believe it when I see it!' Some will say, 'Yes, I believe I indeed will see this manifested, praise GOD!' Both are correct."

"So then, permit the Light dwelling within these pages of truth, honor, love and healings to bear witness that, The Source of All ... (call it what you may) has declared this CITY imprint of love and healing as a gift to the people of the Earth planet."

"The Genii has done her part in allowing us to come forth through her Light Body (electrical system) to share information of massive global change, and she has visual visitation rights into the City of Light, as well of any location including the Embassy of Peace Headquarters."

"Those who has chosen to support this dynamic process, through putting the information into this manuscript form, with their love, talents and intent, and to see it into the hands of the Earth public are to be commended and congratulated, with thanks of Light, even from us in the Embassy Cosmic Community (unseen, but certainly in action.)"

"Today is what it is, tomorrow will be something else quite dramatic and its effects will be felt around the world for peace and healing is the intent and love is the message. MAKE NOTE: This printed document you now hold WILL GO DOWN IN HISTORY as the Pre- Announcement of Coming Attractions. I, OOO-LON, Commander of Space Light and Embassy Interpreter between the Cosmic Community and the Genii declare this to be so ... as stated!"

So Light it Be!

NOTE from Genii. We had thought this visit to the City of Light Embassy of Peace Headquarters would be the last visit included in this edition of the manuscript. Then on the very day that my business partner Charles Betterton was to upload it, I enjoyed yet another visit to the City and I was advised to include it here. There have been many more visits and many more will occur in the future as the City comes forth into this dimension. All relevant visits and updates will be posted to our blog site at http://sedonacityoflight.wordpress.com/.

In the Wonder of It All . . . God Is!

EMBASSY VISIT Saturday Feb 19, 2011

As I enter the scene at a gate of entry, crowds of people are also making their way through it to enjoy what will be an amazing unusual time within the City borders. A hand seen raised above the crowds signals that my City Guide La-Luke is ready to take us into the Embassy of Peace Headquarters via the wheeless trolley.

Upon arrival as we enter, there is a definite audience hum of space conversation reaching our senses. As always, entering this building with the sanctuary of space beings, is always a treat for this lucky lady, and just to be a part of it all is quite an honor. I cannot even imagine what they will teach me, but I am certainly open to learn.

Imagine being in an auditorium with hundreds of friends from many distant locations all sending you love at the same time... Wow! It makes me feel a bit shaky and heart inspired to be a friend that they also enjoy in human attire, and this is even more fun since I decided to be a Jedi with extended love and power attached (plus a lightsaber to play with as light).

Master Yoda's teachings fit in here very well. So standing in front of these five up-close-and-personal entities one could only be great-filled, and I greeted them with an extended bow!

Ooo-lon: "Time for another session is it?"

Genii: "Yes, thank you... a question of the City progress comes to mind, as next week I have a City meeting and any updated information would be of value."

Ooo-lon: "Much progress has been entered into as the City nears. Those of us assembled here have valued the progress as we attune in to your world of energy fields that have been set in place for the readiness of its revelation. Your dimension would be seen, as you have noted, as dense or thick and it needs to be, for the prophecy to be seen and entered into."

"You have been shown that the time warp signals the closeness of the entry. People not knowing of such ways will not have a clue of how this City could be entered into, but they will as time goes on and they get used to the new ways of space technology. Are you following this analogy?"

Genii: "Yes, my interest at this point is what takes place after the City makes its debut? The reaction of people will be quite interesting."

Ooo-lon: "As said, expect a shock wave to spread around the planet for a split second, where the Light of the City can enter minds and fill the place now empty, thus taking people's minds off their daily worries and concerns, no matter what the individual problems would be. The war factor will have men and women standing in such an awareness that to shoot anyone would be not tolerable, as love for one another has taken its place."

"For the Creator of the City and life itself, Call it God, Buddha, Christ or whatever has entered the picture, and due to The City's effects on each one (which of course will vary) nothing will be as it was before. For the Creator has done the impossible in this breathtaking astonishing demonstration."

"Those who are on their knees in praise will connect. Those left will give a standing ovation of utter amazement with the feelings of peace that will quickly sweep around the globe. Have you not asked, what if everyone on the planet felt love all at the same time? This dear one, millions upon millions will experience. Imagine that! as you say quite often."

"Time as you know it will stop as the WORD (as in your 4 Keys of Light sessions) spreads quickly. People may become briefly confused, especially in countries not seeing the City itself in their land location. They may experience it as a heavenly sight in the sky ... as a vision of something new."

"The master Jesus will have many giving him adoration as with the other leaders as well. Likewise, those mentors on higher levels who are adored guides, will be revered as the humans connects with what they feel is their Holy Leader. For nothing less could be mentally evaluated to bring this forth. Indeed this is the greatest show on earth!! It will take a while of sorting out what has taken place, so 'business as usual' will be a thing of the past for a bit, as dramatic changes, change their way of thinking."

"Then will come the celebrations of various degrees as people feel the power and love connected to this unbelievable manifestation of light as it bombards your planet, lighting up the sky and signaling others in the universe that indeed the mission has been accomplished and they too will celebrate in your honor of earth energy accepted."

"The human imagination can only go so far, so this event will enlighten and advance many as they go back to the so called drawing boards ... of thinking new inventive thoughts of success with love the center of it all. For thoughts will only want love to be the leader of whatever they envision through this advancing wisdom from the universe, and the friends they are yet to meet."

"Those into Extraterrestrials will have a field day as the Cosmic Universe has made contact with friends where no man has gone before, as has been advertised. The Universe holds technology to be shared, and no one has to blast off into outer space for, outer space has come to your planet with hands and love extended in healings blessed by the creator. It will be all your yearly celebrations in one."

"Those with demented minds will leave, for they cannot withstand this energy power and pursue the darkness any longer, for indeed the City is too powerful a demonstration for them. Those of light who have worked in believing the highest, will shout Halleluiah! Blessed be for God has spoken and is here and now!"

And with this a roar of applause came from the entities in the back of the auditorium. Is love the answer? OH YES!

Ooo-lon: "Are you at one with this?"

Genii: "Oh yes, a bit overwhelmed but yes.

Ooo-lon: "More questions?"

Genii: "No thank you. I have none at this moment."

Ooo-lon: "In your world this is truth and you depend on the unseen time to produce what has just been said. Has time so called speeded up? Of course as you are well aware. Use it wisely lest it run out." and with this a smile of fun entered his face.

Genii: "Thank you all for being the best friends this planet has ever seen,"

We then departed where a hug at the gate with my guide found me back home watching the clouds dance around the red rocks of Sedona Az.

So Light it Be!

YHVH

With all my Love, Light and Appreciation,

The Genii

Other References to Sedona as a Sacred Site

Sedona's Past, Present and Future As a City of Light

Sedona The City Of Light

In the Cities of Light, there are sacred new cities, crystal palaces, healing temples, Holographic geometrical healing temples of sound and codes of light that have already been created and are anchoring into the Earth from the fifth dimension. In the United States of America, and in many places Globally are preparing for the fifth dimensional shift of consciousness.

The raising of our planet into the new Omega Creation, the Golden Age has arrived. Stargates and corridors are in place here in Sedona, Arizona as well in many other sacred places around the planet. There are many activations and tours offered to assist in the acceleration and group participation.

In many sacred places around the Earth, Venus temples and golden cities are activating. This is part of the divine unfoldment of the Golden age coming, the 7th golden age. In preparation for the amazing events unfolding with each new day, many are guided to participate, fulfilling a sacred agreement made with the creator.

Many of us as a group have done this many times before, and it is our heart's desire to bring heaven to earth. This year 2008 is an accelerated year of unfoldment both inwardly and outwardly. There will be pilgrimages and lay line activation journeys being offered.

http://www.bringingheaventoearth.com/SedonaCrystalCityofLight.html

The History of New Age Sedona as a Sacred Place

Sakina Blue Star, a local woman of Sioux, Choctaw-Cherokee and Scottish heritage, says the Sedona area, once called Nawanda, was traditionally sacred to all tribes of Turtle Island (North America). From all over the continent Native Americans would come for a once-in-a-lifetime journey to seek a vision of what the Great Spirit wanted for their lives.

The area was known as an interdimensional portal. Star People were said to have touched down in ancient times. It was easier for them to come and go here because of the special energies and frequencies. Native Americans kept their contact with other Galactic peoples secret for centuries but now some of them have begun to share their knowledge.

In ancient Lemurian times, Sakina says, Sedona was an island, the Crystal City of Light. People came even then for spiritual enlightenment and learning. Clearly, Sedona has been a center for spiritual seekers for a long time. Since the New Age movement has no central organization, it is not possible to define the phrase in a way which will be acceptable to everyone. However, it can be loosely defined as referring to all of life as sacred and the experience of life as a spiritual journey.

Nicholas Mann, a British visitor trained in the European Geomantic Tradition, wrote a fascinating book called Sedona Sacred Earth, (1989) which details much of the history of the landscape. He studied its lay lines, power centers and vortices, native populations, mythologies, water courses, flora and fauna.

Tracing out a series of sacred patterns among the rock formations which he called geometric landscape temples, he described many individual formations as representing guardians, telling the stories that were associated with them. In the book he drew a parallel with Glastonbury, England. I have felt that connection myself, having visited Glastonbury on four occasions.

http://www.lovesedona.com/01c.htm

Publisher's Note: Sakina Blue Star has recently published an amazing book on her life, Little Dove Lakota Ancestor (www.littledovelakotaancestor.com)

The Sedona Report on Spaceports

Knowing some of you are very interested in connecting into the unseen worlds, I offer the following as perhaps a beginning thought as we progress on our individual paths of advancement. It is a quote from my local Bible these days..(NOTE. if this is not your path of information throw it in the round file).....Genii.

"We are here to offer information about the many Spaceports in the Sedona area. A Spaceport is any place where the connection can be made to what we call...space trails. A space trail is the illusion of a passageway between two points in space. IT IS AN ILLUSION AS, THERE IS NO SUCH THING AS DISTANCE IN SPACE. Distance and separation are both illusionary.

Spaceports within the illusion of space and time are places where one or many can leave whatever dimension they are in and travel to another dimension in another place. There exists a port in the Sedona area for every visual star and many other places in space presently unconscious to human beings. Many sacred sites around the planet are connected to or are access areas Spaceports. Many abandoned sites are connected to Spaceports that are no longer being used. Others are used by nonhuman beings, and the presence of humans is no longer needed at the sight. At this time of the Galactic wave more and more humans will be traveling through the Spaceports in the Sedona area. This is what we call Star traveling. In order to be conscious of these journeys, one must be aware that outer space travel is also inner world travel. The awareness of the stars and constellations in the inner world it is necessary to maintain consciousness while star traveling.

Sedona has volunteered to be a center for the humans who are learning or remembering to star travel. Journeying through the Spaceports it is a necessary part of fulfilling certain responsibilities that the Starseed humans have chosen to take on during this time of transition. There are many places on earth connected to Spaceports. The uniqueness of Sedona is that the Spaceports in this area ARE MORE ACCESSIBLE TO HUMANS and this will be INCREASINGLY SO AS 2012 EVENT APPROACHES IN TIME.

This book **Sedona Starseed** by Raymond Mardyks is a manual for star traveling humans. A guide for both inner and outer travel that few humans up to now were even aware existed. It is a key to freeing oneself from the illusion of space and time." Trans-audio 4-5-2002. The Genii and the Starr-Light have been guided to this book of study for their first introduction into this enormous field of study and education. This geographic location now put you both on the path of Star-study of scientific events to come to pass. We who guide the star embedded students welcome you and those who also will be tapped to follow..."

Sedona and The Celestine Prophecy by James Redfield

The Celestine Prophecy: An Adventure by James Redfield
In the rain forests of Peru, an ancient manuscript has been discovered. Within its pages are 9 key insights into life itself -- insights each human being is predicted to grasp sequentially, one insight then another, as we move toward a completely spiritual culture on Earth.

The Celestine Prophecy tells a gripping story of adventure and discovery, but is also a guidebook that has the power to crystallize your perceptions of why you are where you are in life--and to direct your steps with a new energy and optimism as you head into tomorrow.

This adventure parable is one of modern publishing's greatest success stories. The Celestine Prophecy spent over 3 years on the *New York Times* best sellers list and appeared on lists around the world. It was the #1 international bestseller of 1996 (#2 in 1995); in 1995 and 1996, it was the #1 American book in the world. www.celestinevision.com

" Feeling "kind of stuck" at one point, Redfield went to the high-energy vortexes of Sedona, Arizona-an area that he and many others regard as a sacred place. As he recounts in an interview in *Body, Mind, Spirit* magazine: "I was sitting on a ridge near the Chapel Vortex and trying to work with the notes for the book. It was not coming easily. All of a sudden, a crow flew out of the canyon and right over my head and then flew back into the canyon. I continued to make notes. I was having some trouble getting the story to flow out. The crow came out of the canyon again and flew over me, then back into the canyon, so I went into the canyon, and when I sat down the book just came pouring out."   http://www.celestinevision.com/jr_bio.html.

Redfield's books are included in the featured resources.

Sacred Sites, Sedona by Shirley MacLaine

The majestic beauty of the Red Rocks of Sedona are indeed breath-taking. But it is not just the scenery that attracts thousands of visitors each year. In fact, the land around the city of Sedona holds two major attractions: a rich history as a sacred site and vortex energy.

The original inhabitants considered the land sacred, as do many of the present day indigenous people in the area. Our ancestors under-stood the principles of the physics of the Earth and revered Earth energy, which they could feel and sense, as a gift from the Creator. The energy, the gift from the Creator, is what made the land sacred to them.

Ancient spiritual petro glyphs decorate the walls of caves and canyons, reminding the present day visitors that this is very old ritualistic land and should be respected as such. Medicine Wheels, some authentic, some not, are sprinkled across sandstone mesas northeast of Sedona.

These decorations, whether old or new, are symbolic of a desire for a connection to Creation and Nature. However, the symbolic decoration of the land is not the attaching bond to either Creation or Nature. In fact, the bond to the visible reality of Creation and Nature is found in the unseen... the energy.

The majority of people traveling to Sedona are drawn to the land because of its energy vortices or vortexes. Some people don't even know why they are there, until they experience this energy. A classic case of this unseen force can be found at Bell Rock, considered one of the major vortices in the area and an excellent example of an electromagnetic vortex. Easily accessible off of highway 179, just a few miles south of Sedona and north of Oak Creek Village, this magnificent red sandstone butte almost beckons people to it.

The locals suggest that you try vortex energy experiment. Some of you will want to travel to this area for the experience. If you do go to Bell Rock, try these experiments then ask yourself what you are feeling. For those of you that can feel the energy through the vibrational frequency of the words Sedona and Bell Rock, try the experiments right now and ask yourself, "What am I feeling?".

Carefully climb the slopes of Bell Rock. Sit quietly in a meditative state for a few minutes. Then gently rub the palms of your hands together as this increases the sensitivity to their reception. Hold you arms straight on either side of your body with your palms facing down.

This land and this particular vortex are considered activators and quite often people feel a tremendous connection to the land and to their past incarnations. Visitors sometimes recognize this past-life experiential energy and suddenly feel like they have found their home, a reaction that is common with many sacred sites around the world.

Sometimes this particular experiment brings up such vivid past-life memories that the individuals begin to cry; partially because they have broken through a personal barrier and partially because this type of recall is such an emotional release.

There is a second part to this experiment. Hold your arms straight out to your side with the palms of your hands facing upwards. You may experience a momentary surge of energy and weightlessness. People often report that they felt their arms being lifted toward the heavens and an opening of their seventh chakra. In this case, the experience rarely cries. Instead, their sense of joy and happiness brings about an ear to ear smile and laughter.

The experiences garnered from both portions of the experiment, the palms up and palms down, are beneficial to one's spiritual growth. But, it is important to remember that not every sacred site affects every individual. Nor will all people react to the energy in the same way.

The vortex centers of Sedona, which include Bell Rock, Cathedral Rock, Boynton Canyon, Long Canyon and Airport Mesa, are also said to emit a melodic frequency that is soothing to the soul. This harmonic frequency can also be experienced on the slopes of Bell Rock. Sit quietly. Become accustomed to the wind against the cliffs and then listen with your heart.

You may hear the frequencies of the spiraling vortex or you may hear your Higher Self and spend the afternoon in a delightful internal dialogue that includes you, your Higher Self, Nature and Creation.

http://www.shirleymaclaine.com/articles/sites/article-314

Appreciation for Shirley MacLaine

If we had to recommend only one book, movie or television program to help validate (or at least help explain) the foundation of what is being shared in this publication, it would be the Shirley MacLaine's classic, **Out On A Limb**.

ABC aired a 4-hour mini-series in 1987 and a few copies are usually available on the web. There is also an Australian DVD also for sale but it won't play on most DVD players in the US.

We found that **Out On A Limb** contained far more wisdom and practical guidance on how to awaken, get in touch with your true identity and discover the much larger universe we dwell in than The Secret.

Shirley MacLaine stepped "out on a limb" in ways that benefited all of human kind. She had the courage to open doors of enlightened consciousness that the world is now able and more ready to hear and appreciate her wisdom.

Therefore, we are encouraging Shirley and Brit Elders, her CEO for Shirley MacLaine.com, to consider taking **Out On A Limb** to the big screen. Please do join us in the campaign by sending a message of support and interest to them at http://www.shirleymaclaine.com/. You will also be able to order books, CD's and DVD's from Shirley.

 **Sage-ing While Age-ing Book and CD**	 **Inner Power DVD** Journey Within Program for Stress Reduction and Relaxation Through Meditation.	 **Out On A Limb** Five hours of Shirley sharing her amazing life changing story on audio cassettes

:

Loving the Planet and Each Other

An Interview with Ken Carey by Randy Peyser
(Copyright Randy Peyser. Reprinted with permission)

Ken Carey is the author of "**The Starseed Transmission**," "**Vision, Return of the Bird Tribes**," "**Flatrock Journal**" and "**The Third Millennium**."

Randy Peyser: Where do you get your information when you write your books? Is it all channeled to you?

Ken Carey: Well, I don't channel in the sense that many do. It's not a process of my ego stepping aside, and some foreign entity taking over and speaking through me. I'm a full participant in the process, both in terms of my spirit and my ego.

I relax into a larger experience of being. It's a matter of taking that sense of self that we call the ego and not denying or rejecting it, but relaxing it...relaxing its interpretations of the world around us, relaxing its definitions, relaxing its defenses. When I relax into this larger experience of being, I find that my heart increasingly opens in love. I have a saying that "I can understand anything that I can love."

I speak about this in my newest book, *The Third Millennium*. For me the process of opening up to a larger field of awareness is a process of beginning to love everything immediately around me. I begin with my body, my clothes, the chair I'm sitting on if I'm indoors, or the rock I'm sitting on if I'm outside, or the tree I may be leaning against.

The more I'm able to love, the more I realize that all of this is part of me. We're all cells in the same whole. We're all parts of the same beautiful planetary organism.

There does come a point sometimes, not always, when my love just opens up like this. I feel this awareness and especially the creative force of the life of this earth. I feel a love that is so indescribable I can't help but try to put it into words now and again.

RP: A lot of times before opening to love, there's fear.

KC: There's fear because opening to love can be a scary process. There is no dishonesty in love. If you think of the life force in your body as a current of love, it's like a brilliant light. When that light shines, the shadows become darker and more distinct.

Opening to love helps us to see where we have not been honest with ourselves, or games we might be playing. People sometimes are scared of that, but it's nothing to be afraid of. I like to see things that I may be doing that inhibit the flow of creativity in my life, so I welcome the process. There are times I see things I'd rather not see, but I'm glad I do because it indicates an area where I need to change to become a more loving person.

RP: How do you feel we're doing as a planet in terms of opening?

KC: We're right on schedule and I think we're doing amazingly well. When I wrote *The Starseed Transmission* in 1978, the world was such a tremendously different place. The changes since then have been phenomenal. The *Starseed Transmission* spoke about major global, political and economic changes taking place between the years 1987 and 1989 and it was between those years that the Berlin Wall came down and Eastern Europe was freed, apartheid ended in South Africa, and the Soviet Union collapsed. So wonderful things have been happening.

I know there are still problems. The break up of the old polarized communist versus free world has created a whole new set of problems, but they're becoming more manageable. They're becoming problems on a scale that we can creatively address and solve. The tendency of the media is to focus on the negative simply because the negative results in reportable events alot more than the positive does. But despite the media, there's no doubt in my mind, just on the basis of the people I meet and my own experience, that the world is infinitely more conscious now than it was a decade or two ago. And that process is only going to continue. In fact, I believe it is accelerating more rapidly than before.

RP: That sounds very positive. You sound very hopeful.

KC: You have to be. It's not that I don't have my own doubts from time to time. I certainly do. But I know deep down that we've embarked on a wonderful adventure. And while no one can predict all the twists and turns that the road before us may take, I know the destination that it's leading to. I've seen it. I've lived it, and it's here now for those who are willing to release the past programming, the fear, the judgment, and the prejudice that gets in the way of seeing it.

RP: Can you talk a little about what that destination looks like to you?

KC: I see it simply as a state in which our human family exists without shooting ourselves in the foot every five minutes, and without exceeding our own purposes and engaging in so much counter-productive activity.

Humans have been abusive to one another, to the planet and to other species. The future that I write about in The Third Millennium is the time when we will realize that it is not in our best interest to solve a disagreement through armed conflict when we could negotiate instead. We'll begin to realize that much of our historical behavior is simply no longer viable and obviously never was useful.

This is already being realized increasingly. I think the creativity that we'll be able to express as a species will be so beautiful. I see the potential. And it's not just potential; it is being manifested in many places. There are groups that are working to feed the hungry in inner cities. People all over are showing that there is a way that we can exist on this planet, in love with one another and the earth and other creatures. I just see this spreading and becoming increasingly the norm.

RP. What do you think about all the predictions about earth changes?

KC: There have always been earth changes. I think there will be more than there have been in the past. Whether they're cataclysmic depends a lot on us. I don't think they necessarily have to be harmful.

Last year or the year before, in Missouri, we had big floods. My heart went out to all those farmers who got flooded out along the Mississippi River. But at the same time I thought, it flooded this way in the twenties, it flooded this way in the fifties, and they've built their homes on a flood plain. If it floods occasionally, they've got to expect that.

There's not enough respect for nature. A lot of what we see as cataclysmic is simply the earth telling us, "Look, you've got to honor me more. You've got to honor the nature of this flood plain." This is reality and this is part of what the earth needs, North America needs, to cleanse herself. We can't stop it because it happens in good, good fertile ground.

If you want to grow crops down here, grow them down here, but build your house up on the hill. It's the same with the hurricane in Dade County, Florida. It was heart-breaking to see what those people experienced. But that land was never meant to be packed with so many dwellings.

There's a certain sense of the earth and what it's for that I see coming into our awareness. The government's talking about no longer continuing federally subsidized flood insurance for places that flood regularly. This is a good sign. It shows that we're beginning to pay more attention to the landscape so that ultimately our buildings can be better. Some architects are already creating structures that are designed to be a part of the earth, to respect a local watershed, the nature of the soil, the rainfall and the climactic conditions. It's this sort of increasing respect for the earth that many of these natural disasters are guiding us towards and leading us to. I think it's the earth's way of saying, "Hey, have you forgotten somebody here?"

RP: Any last thoughts you'd like to share?

KC: Yes. I'd like to emphasize that the way we look at things, our favorite view points, our favorite concepts, the images that we use to describe reality to ourselves, our religions, our belief systems, and our politics are of no more eternal significance than the color of the clothes we wear from day to day.

If these things help us become more loving, conscious people, if they help us become more aware of the miraculous nature of the planetary life that surrounds us, and if they help us to be more creative, then they're good. I don't care what continent they come from, what cultures they're steeped in or what beliefs they involve. If they help us do those things, they're positive. This helps me to remember what I tend to forget sometimes — it helps me remember what a miraculous universe I live in.

There will be those who can relate to *The Third Millennium* and those who can't, but I think the most important thing is that we respect the paths that our sisters and brothers are on, whatever form they take, because ultimately it is our love for one another and our union that is going to bring about the greatest and most beneficial planetary changes.

We'll never agree on the level of the mind. We're never going to agree on a belief system or a conceptual framework. But we can already agree in our hearts, simply because we are humans, and we are living together in an incredible world on the brink of a new and wondrous era.

RP: We're all in this together.

KC: That's right. There's no doubt about it.

PLEASE NOTE: Many people contact Randy Peyser who want to contact Ken Carey. This interview took place in the mid '90's and Randy no longer has his contact information. www.RandyPeyser.com.

Ken Carey's books are included in the Featured Resources

A Second Age of Universal Creation

From The Third Millennium – Living in the Post Historic World by Ken Carey

I would have you first know the spirit of God through one another, through your human families, and then through the creatures of the world: through the four-footed and the winged, the fish that swim the ocean depths, the vegetation that blossoms in every healthy environment. I would have you know me through the many. In these realms this is how I know myself.

I come to this world not to know myself as the One, for that I have always known, but to know myself in you, to perceive a world through your eyes, that together we might continue the work of creation and together enjoy all that has been created.

One identity wave flows through all that is, from the universal to the personal. It splashes upon these temporal shores, leaving behind in its creative wake the luminous droplets of individuality that becomes all creatures, both of the spirit world and of the world of form. This wave is the current of my eternal love. It carries an intelligence I invite you to share, to remember as your own.

I speak to you through these transmissions at times through the perspectives of the many, through the angelic beings who know their source in my wholeness. At other times I speak to you as the One, as your Creator and your Source.

The manner of speaking in the first person recognizes the distinction between human egos and the spirit of God. Even as the cells are distinguished from the body, these are distinguished. Yet this manner of address is not intended to distinguish human spirits from my own. All spirit comes from and returns to the same source. I share this first-person account not to diminish your awareness of that source but to heighten it, perhaps even to remembrance.

To let your ego stand alone while you and I converse as two-this is education. And it is good. But to feel your ego revived and alive again as together in oneness we experience the terrestrial world-this is creation. This is bliss itself, a joining more wonderful than any sexual union. It reactivates the mechanism that brings my focused attention, and therefore new creation, to the earth. It brings the human ego refreshment from the deepest truth, fulfilling every purpose, every longing, every season for its being.

For your ego and my spirit are eternal lovers. Throughout these many thousands of years of history, human egos have longed for my presence as I have longed for their return to their place in Creation's design. But they have been blind to my presence.

They have known only fleeting snatches of the love I bring, if they have known it at all. Yet I have guided your race along a measured path that has at last brought you here today, to this moment when communication between us is clear and conscious.

The love song that enters your awareness as you turn your heart again to your source comes a loving current of attentive energy. As you accept that love, you feel how thoroughly you are loved by the Creator who has called you into being. You become immersed in that love. You feel it even as it is felt for you, even as it brings into being all that you perceive and encounter.

You are the species through whom I love creation and the means through which I shall call out her greater potential. You are my gift to the world and the world's return to me. Wherever this material plane has not yet blossomed into the fullness of her potential, your love will provide a climate for that blossoming; your thoughts and actions will provide the nutrients for its growth.

As you allow yourself to receive fully my love for you, you become capable of loving as I do. Through that love you become a conscious cell in my dimensional body of thought and expression, while retaining your human body and your individuality of form, you simultaneously know yourself in spirit as one with your Creator. However, the individual is never the whole of God.

The God, that lives within you lives also within all of humankind, though in some I am honored and in some I am denied. My spirit manifests in all biological life, in all planetary life, in all stellar life, in all things from the greatest spiraling galaxy to the tiniest subatomic particle.

Each creature is designed to specialize its expression of certain of my attributes, bringing to focus my specific qualities and characteristics. This is how, and why, individuals are created. As I proceed now in the final stages of awakening in the collective consciousness of your race, there are individuals beginning to realize the greater truth who yet confuse the point of saying, "I am God."

There is no need for such a statement More often than not it causes confusion. The very mouth that forms the words proclaims that the speaker is-if awakened- an individualized expression of God, a part of God, a servant of God, a representative of God, one with God in spirit. But the human form that individual inhabits a world of many diverse and spiritually equal beings, no one whom is greater than another.

Those who share my consciousness throughout the earth and working most closely with me in facilitating planetary awakening, those who are healing and educating, are no greater than those who are not. Even those who give other cause to fear are not spiritually inferior, only sleeping still-as perhaps you yourself slept not so long ago.

Though some may be among the wheat I gather up into the harvest of this age and others among the chaff that will be filtered out and assigned to a realm of continuing education, even between these there is no spiritual distinction. Among those who are consciously sharing my presence, there is no greater or lesser, no master or servant, no lords or commoners.

All are equal in the eyes of God, but those who are awakened and those immersed in the educational process that lead to awakening. After my awakening in collective human consciousness, the creative pursuits of awakened human beings will be far more varied than the roles played in the historical era, yet there will be no hierarchy or ruling class. You will know yourself as a family, sharing the enjoyment, the awareness, the exploration of these dimensional frequencies, working together in spiritual equality to develop their potential.

The Near Death Experience and the City of Light

Kevin Williams' Research Conclusions. Copyright 2008. Reprinted with permission

Fifty of the near-death experiences I profile on this website which I gathered statistics on, 17% of them experienced a city of light. These cities of light have been described by various experiencers using such adjectives as: golden, beautiful, unearthly, fairy tale-like, indescribable, beyond anything that can be described, so superior to anything on earth, colorful, brilliant, heavenly, endless, crystalline, grand, paradise, and galaxy-like.

- These cities of light are said by experiencers to represent an entire world, made of light and love, radiate with multi-colored lights, with transcendental music, filled with light beings, made of glass, built of the purest light, multi-dimensional, built by God, whose light of the city is God, the city of God, resembling New Jerusalem, the heavenly city in the Book of Revelation.

- Within the city of lights, experiencers have seen glowing crystal cathedrals, domes, towers like European castles, and houses like never seen on earth.

- This city of light experienced by some Christian experiencers have been identified to be the New Jerusalem, a heavenly city described in the Book of Revelation in the Bible. According to Revelation, this city comes down from heaven to the earth sometime in the future. Because the Book of Revelation is highly symbolic, it might be that this city described in the Bible is also symbolic.

NDE References of a City of Light

- **A golden city with towers and domes:**

Just a little ways off I could see a bridge with someone standing on it. Beyond the bridge, I saw a golden city with towers like European castles. The whole city seemed to be shining with light that shot up into the sky like a giant searchlight. I could see that some of the domes of the city were red, others were gold, and a few were blue. The gates and walls of the city seemed to be made of bright blue, red, and violet lights. (Randy Gehling)

- **A city of crystal cathedrals:**

Like wingless birds, we swept into a city of cathedrals. These cathedrals were made entirely of a crystalline substance that glowed with a light that shone powerfully from within. I was awestruck. This place had a power that seemed to pulsate through the air. I knew that I was in a place of learning. I wasn't there to witness my life or to see what value it had had, I was there to be instructed.

(Dannion Brinkley)

- **A beautiful unearthly city:**

Jesus took Emanuel back to heaven and showed him a beautiful city. Emanuel said this was a very beautiful city with houses he has never seen anywhere in the world. There was a lake there and he was told he could not go across it. (Emanuel Tuwagirairmana)

- **A beautiful fairy tale city:**

I remember the scene was shown to me in a fairy tale city and setting - somewhat like I had always wished for in my life while alive. It was so beautiful. (Sherry Gideon)

- **A city that represents a world:**

As I found myself at the top of the hill, I saw that over on the horizon and just a little bit lower on the horizon, there was a city. I realized in some way that this was more than just a city, that what I was seeing actually represented a world. I wondered, "Was that the world I just came from or the one I am going to? (Jayne Smith)

- **A multi-colored crystal city:**

In the distance I saw a sight so magnificent and astounding - a city made up of what seemed to be glass or crystal! The lights were of many colors that radiated from it. Never have I ever seen such a sight! I began walking toward the city in a daze of unbelief! So many questions raced through my mind. I had to know where I was. What was happening to me? I reached the front of the city and saw a double door that looked to be about thirty feet or so in height and width! (Ricky Randolph)

- **Souls are seen being prepared for the city of light:**

Those living on the higher realms of the city radiate the brightest light, being so resplendent that their glory must be cloaked so others of lower degree can look upon them. Visiting the higher levels is possible, but the spirits of lower realms must be prepared or covered so they can stand in the presence of greater glory.

... Some new arrivals are taken to a place of orientation where they rest, adjust to their new condition, and prepare to take their place in the city of light. (Craig Lundahl)

Dr. George Ritchie's City of Light Experience

An endless, brilliant, city of light and love:

And then I saw, infinitely far off, far too distant to be visible with any kind of sight I knew of- a city. A glowing, seemingly endless city, bright enough to be seen over all the unimaginable distance between. The brightness seemed to shine from the very walls and streets of this place, and from beings which I could now discern moving about within it. In fact, the city and everything in it seemed to be made of light, even as the figure at my side was made of light.

At this time I had not yet read the Book of Revelation. I could only gape in awe at this faraway spectacle, wondering how bright each building, each inhabitant, must be to be seen over so many light-years of distance. Could these radiant beings, I wondered, amazed, be those who had indeed kept Jesus the focus of their lives? Was I seeing at last ones who had looked for him in everything? Looked so well and so closely that they had been changed into his very likeness? Even as I asked the question, two of the bright figures seemed to detach themselves from the city and start toward us, hurling themselves across that infinity with the speed of light.

Now this was surprising because this was the first realm in which the inhabitants could see the Christ and me. Even more amazing, they exuded light almost as brilliant as the Christ. As the two beings approached us, I could also feel the love flowing from them toward us. The complete joy they showed at seeing the Christ was unmistakable.

Seeing these beings and feeling the joy, peace and happiness which swelled up from them made me feel that here was the place of all places, the top realm of all realms. The beings who inhabited it were full of love. This, I was and am convinced, is heaven. As marvelous as I thought the previous realm was, after glimpsing this new realm we were seeing, I began to understand for the first time what Paul was saying in 1 Corinthians 13 when he wrote: "If I have the gift of prophecy and can fathom all mysteries and all knowledge, and if I have a faith that can remove mountains, but have not love, I am nothing."

I do not infer that the wonderful souls of the fourth realm did not have love because they did but not to the degree that the souls of this realm had reached.

But as fast as they came toward us, we drew away. Desperately I cried out to him not to leave me, to make me ready for that shining city, not to abandon me in this dark and narrow place. (Dr. George Ritchie)

David Oakford's City of Light Experience

A heavenly city in the clouds where souls leave to come to earth and where souls go for after death for rejuvenation:

[Webmaster's note: David Oakford uses the name Gaia, the real name of this planet. For ease of reading, I have replaced his references of Gaia with earth.]

We started to head back toward earth. We went to a place in the shadow of earth. It was a great city in the clouds. The city had these beautiful white buildings as far as I could see. I saw spirits living there all of which had vibration but no real physical body. These inhabitants went to and from the buildings - going to work and play too. I saw a place where spirits went to get what I thought was water. There were no vehicles there. Spirits seemed to get around the same way my being and I got around, by flying.

The city had no boundaries that I could see. This was a place full of life of all kinds. There was nature there, many pure plants, trees, and water just like on earth but more pure. Nature there was absolutely perfect. It was untainted by human manipulation. This place was just like earth only without the problems and negativity. I felt that this was what is called heaven in earth terms.

I saw spirits going to and from earth and the city. I could tell the development of the spirits going to and from by the energy they emanated. I could see that animals came to and from earth just like humans do. I could see many spirits leave earth with guides and could see spirits returning to earth without guides. The being told me that some of the spirits passing were the ones that were doing the work with humans on earth . I could make out the type of spirits that were doing the work and the spirits that were coming to the great city to become replenished to eventually go back to earth to experience and further evolve. I could feel the emotions of the ones coming back for replenishment. I could feel that some of them were sad, beaten and scared, much like I felt before my being came to me. (David Oakford)

NDE References of a Multi-Dimensional City of Light

Jan Price's NDE (You can buy Jan Price's book **The Other Side of Death** at www.quartus.org)

- **A multi-dimensional city of increasing glory**:

Taking form before my eyes was the skyline of a great city. I could see three different dimensions of it simultaneously. The first had a dinginess pervading the atmosphere. There was a gloominess, and everything was gray, even the inhabitants, though I sensed that somewhere beneath the discoloration pulsed life and beauty. It brought to mind the lowest levels of existence in the world from which I'd come. Evil walked the squalid streets with malevolent bearing. No one here was up to, or expected, any good.

The second dimension was of the same panorama, but brighter and more colorful, and had a familiarity. Hope lived amid despair. There were neighborhoods with neat houses holding reasonably contented folk; shabby rows of dwellings housed those more discontented. Expansive lawns separated palatial homes from those of less grandeur. Within each sector was happiness and horror, love and hate, joy and sorrow -the dualities of life on a less that harmonious plane. It was a life accepted by many in the land I'd left behind as the only way life could be. Some knew better, more than just a few, and the hope that lived amid despair would at some time blossom into a better way of life.

Last in the trinity was a city of light, like unto John's holy city in the Book of Revelation. I saw the same skyline as before, but this time it was pure gold - with colors like precious gems, transparent glass, crystal clear. All who walked through the city brought glory and honor into it. Harmony and order prevailed, and the residents lived joyfully, creating that which brought forth beauty and fulfillment- a place of perfect peace, the peace that passes understanding. (Jan Price)

Dr. Craig Lundahl's City of Light Research

Dr. Craig Lundahl is one of the pioneers in NDE research. Together with Dr. Harold A. Widdison, their research is documented in their classic NDE book entitled, The Eternal Journey. This book divulges mesmerizing eyewitness descriptions of the hereafter's city of light. Information they gleaned from experiencers suggests that the afterlife has two major divisions. The first division has been named cities of light by Dr. Raymond Moody, Betty Eadie, Dr. Melvin Morse, and others. The other division has been variously labeled a realm of bewildered spirits by Moody, a place devoid of love by Dr. George Ritchie, a place of earthbound/lingering spirits by Eadie, and the sphere of wasted, elusive, and misused opportunities by Joy Snell. Here are some examples from their book:

- **Heavenly cities of increasing glory:**

In a moment we were at the gates of a beautiful city. A porter opened it and we passed in. They city was grand and beautiful beyond anything that I can describe. It was clothed in the purest light, brilliant but not glaring or unpleasant. The people, men and women, in their employments and surroundings seemed contented and happy. I knew those I met without being told who they were. My guide would not permit me to pause much by the way, but rather hurried me on through this place to another still higher but connected with it. It was still more beautiful and glorious than anything I had before seen. To me its extent and magnificence were incomprehensible. This man visited three unique places, a place where people were yet to reach their assigned place, a city of light, and a second city of even greater grandeur beyond the previous city of light. He pleaded with his guide to remain and was told he was "permitted only to visit these heavenly cities, for I had not filled my mission in yonder world; therefore I must return and take my body." (Dr. Craig Lundahl)

- **More heavenly cities of increasing glory:**

John Powell had a similar experience when, in his words:

> A personage came and said, "Come!"
>
> My spirit left my body and went with my guide who took me to the next planet. Here I beheld the inhabitants. The houses and trees were beautiful to behold. I was so amazed and delighted that I requested my guide to permit me to stay and dwell there, for all things were far superior and in advance of this world that I had come from.
>
> He answered, "No," and said, "Come."
>
> He then took me to the next kingdom which so exceeded the first in beauty and glory that I was again amazed and requested permission to stay. I cannot command language to describe the beauty of the inhabitants and scenery, but my guide said, "No, come!"
>
> He then took me to the next kingdom which was far more beautiful in glory and order than the former two. The beautiful flowers, trees, gardens, people who were dressed in pure white, and so pure that I was overwhelmed with joy and
> most earnestly implored my guide to allow me to stay, but he said, "You cannot go any further, for this is next to the throne of God." (Dr. Craig Lundahl)

- **Even more heavenly cities of increasing glory:**

Herr Pettersson was also permitted to visit the spirit world and discovered, much to his surprise, that even the worst in heaven exceeded the best on earth. To Herr Pettersson the world of spirits resembled the material world. There were many countries, or kingdoms. There were cities and villages, temples and palaces, flowers and animals of great beauty and variety. The people were very busy. Some were preaching on street corners and in assembly halls, and all had great congregations. But no matter what level or city a person qualifies for, each city is so superior to any on earth that it is indescribable, and each succeeding realm is indescribably better than that immediately below it. It seems that the assignment to a specific city is contingent on the actions and attitudes of the individual while on earth. The key that opens the gate to a specific city of light is the ability to dwell in the light of that city, and this evidently depends on behaviors during earth life. (Dr. Craig Lundahl)

Edgar Cayce's NDE

- **A journey through a tunnel of cities of increasing glory:**

I am conscious of a white beam of light, knowing that I must follow it or be lost. As I move along this path of light I gradually become conscious of various levels upon which there is movement. Upon the first levels there are vague, horrible shapes, grotesque forms such as one sees in nightmares. Passing on, there begins to appear on either side misshapen forms of human beings with some part of the body magnified. Again there is change and I become conscious of gray-hooded forms moving downward. Gradually, these become lighter in color.

Then the direction changes and these forms move upward and the color of the robes grows rapidly lighter. Next, there begins to appear on either side vague outlines of houses, walls, trees, etc., but everything is motionless. As I pass on, there is more light and movement in what appear to be normal cities and towns. With the growth of movement I become conscious of sounds, at first indistinct rumblings, then music, laughter, and singing of birds. There is more and more light, the colors become very beautiful, and there is the sound of wonderful music. The houses are left behind; ahead there is only a blending of sound and color. Quite suddenly I come upon a Hall of Records. It is a hall without walls, without ceiling, but I am conscious of seeing an old man who hands me a large book, a record of the individual for whom I seek information. (Edgar Cayce)

NDE References of Cities of Light

- **Cities of light with beautiful music:**

In the bardo of becoming, as well as many other kinds of visions, the mental body will see visions and signs of different realms. A small percentage of those who have survived a near-death experience report visions of inner worlds, paradises, and cities of light with transcendental music. (Lingza Chokyi)

- **Cities of colorful light:**

A long way off there was a pinprick of light. I moved toward it, slowly at first, then faster and faster as if I were on top of a train accelerating. Then I stopped and stepped fully into the light. I noticed everything - sky, buildings, glass - emitted its own light and everything was much more colorful than what we see here. A river meandered around. On the other side was a city, and a road running through it to another city, and another city and another and another ... The first city was like first grade. People stayed there until they were ready to go to the next city - your eternal progression, from city to city. (Cecil)

- **Cities built of light:**

Darryl, [a] man who was electrocuted when his home was struck by lightning, found himself moving toward lights. As he drew closer to the lights he realized they were cities and that the cities were built of light. (Dr. Craig Lundahl)

- **Golden cities:**

Others have reported seeing children playing in big golden cities and seeing busy people in cities, from which it is possible to infer there is more than one city in the spirit world. (Dr. Craig Lundahl)

NDE References of a City of Light Resembling a Galaxy

- **A galaxy-like city of lights:**

In its total energy configuration, the galaxy looked like a fantastic city of lights. (Mellen-Thomas Benedict)

- **A galaxy of light beings:**

We started going faster and faster, out of the darkness. Embraced by the light, feeling wonderful and crying, I saw off in the distance something that looked like the picture of a galaxy, except that it was larger and there were more stars than I had seen on earth. There was a great center of brilliance. In the center there was an enormously bright concentration. Outside the center countless millions of spheres of light were flying about entering and leaving what was a great being-ness at the center. It was off in the distance ...

Everywhere around us were countless radiant beings, like stars in the sky, coming and going. It was like a super magnified view of a galaxy super packed with stars. And in the giant radiance of the center they were packed so densely together that individuals could not be identified. Their selves were in such harmony with the Creator that they were really just one. (Rev. Howard Storm)

Emanuel Swedenborg's References to "Heavenly Communities"

- **Souls visit various heavenly cities to determine their residence:**

So they are taught by their friends about the state of eternal life, and are taken around to different places, into different communities. Some are taken to cities, some to gardens and parks; but most are taken to splendid places because this sort of place delights the outward nature they are still involved in.

Then they are intermittently led into thoughts they had during their physical life about the soul's state after death, heaven, and hell, until they also come to resent their former utter ignorance of things like this, and resent the Church's ignorance of such matters. (Emanuel Swedenborg)

- **Swedenborg's writings about the cities of light:**

Two hundred years ago Emanuel Swedenborg was writing about the same common elements found in NDEs. In his writings he frequently mentions the feelings of ineffability and also the peace and joy. He speaks of a light which he calls the Sun of Heaven. He tells us stories of those who meet their friends or relatives who had died before them. He speaks of the review of the person's life, the cities of light, and the realm of frustrated spirits. He even speaks about the out-of-body experience before there was any public knowledge of such a thing. (Emanuel Swedenborg website)

- **Swedenborg's discussion of how a soul's destination to a particular heavenly community is determined:**

Taken all together, they [our desires] make up a kind of kingdom. Thus they are in fact organized within a person, even though people are completely unaware of their organization. To some extent, however, this is made known to people in the other life where they have an outreach of thought and affection that depends on this organization. This is an outreach into the heavenly communities if the strongest desire is made up of desires of heaven, but an outreach into hellish communities if the strongest desire is made up of desires of hell.

This has been made clear to me by observed experiences over and over again. The whole of heaven is divided into communities on the basis of differences in the good that comes from desire. Every single spirit who is raised into heaven and becomes an angel is taken to the community where his or her desire is, and once there they are where they belong, so to speak- as though they were at home, where they were born.

An angel senses this, and makes close friends with others like themselves. When they leave and go to another community, there is a certain constant resistance. This is the effect of their longing to return to those who are like themselves, which means to their own strongest desire. This is how close friendships are formed in heaven. The same holds true in hell, where people also form friendships on the basis of desires which are opposed to heavenly ones.

Paths are visible in the spiritual world. Some lead to heaven, some to hell; one to one community, one to another. Good spirits travel only along paths that lead to heaven, to the community which is involved in the particular good that comes from their own desire. They do not see paths leading in other directions.

Evil spirits follow only paths that lead to hell, to the particular community there which is involved in the evil that comes from their own desire. They do not see paths leading in other directions; and even if they do, they do not want to follow them.

All souls arrive at the type of community where their spirits were in the physical world. In fact every person is bonded to a particular heavenly or hellish community - -an evil person to a hellish one, a good person to a heavenly one. A person is guided there step-by-step and eventually gains entrance.

When evil people are involved in the state of their more inward elements, they are turned by stages toward their own community. Eventually they are turned straight toward it before this state is completed. And once this state is completed, they hurl themselves into the hell where there are people like themselves.

The separation of the good from the evil happens in various ways. Broadly, it happens by taking the evil ones around to those communities they were in touch with through their good thoughts and affections during their first state. In this way, they are taken to those communities which were persuaded by their outward appearance that they were not evil. Normally, they are taken on an extensive circuit, and everywhere they are exposed as they really are to good souls. On seeing them, the good souls turn away, and as they turn away, the evil souls who are being taken around also turn their faces away from the good ones and turn toward the region of hellish communities, which is their destination.
(Emanuel Swedenborg)

Biblical References of a "Heavenly City"

A city built by God:

> For he was looking forward to the city with foundations, whose architect and builder is God. (Heb. 11:10)

Choosing the city of God instead of reincarnation:

> If they had been thinking of the country they had left, they would have had opportunity to return. Instead, they were longing for a better country - a heavenly o ne. Therefore God is not ashamed to be called their God, for he has prepared a city for them. (Heb. 11:13-16)

- **An eternal city:**

    For here we do not have an enduring city, but we are looking for the city that is to come. (Heb. 13:14)

- **The New Jerusalem - the city of God:**

    I will write on him the name of my God and the name of the city of my God, the new Jerusalem, which is coming down out of heaven from my God. (Rev. 3:12)

- **Earth becomes a city of God:**

    I saw the Holy City, the new Jerusalem, coming down out of heaven from God, prepared as a bride beautifully dressed for her husband. And I heard a loud voice from the throne saying, "Now the dwelling of God is with men, and he will live with them. They will be his people, and God himself will be with them and be their God." (Rev. 21:2-3)

- **A crystal city of light:**

    ... the Holy City, Jerusalem, coming down out of heaven from God. It shone with the glory of God, and its brilliance was like that of a very precious jewel, like a jasper, clear as crystal. (Rev. 21:10-11)

- **The light of the city is God:**

    I did not see a temple in the city, because the Lord God Almighty and the Lamb are its temple. The city does not need the sun or the moon to shine on it, for the glory of God gives it light, and the Lamb is its lamp. The nations will walk by its light, and the kings of the earth will bring their splendor into it. On no day will its gates ever be shut, for there will be no night there. The glory and honor of the nations will be brought into it. Nothing impure will ever enter it, nor will anyone who does what is shameful or deceitful, but only those whose names are written in the Lamb's book of life. (Rev. 21:22-27)

Fourteen Etheric Cities of the Earth

The Fourteen Etheric Cities are real cities in the Etheric Realm of our planet Earth, located over seven deserts or continents and over seven large bodies of water. Certain Ascended Masters and Divine Beings and sometimes some unascended beings serve in these Etheric Cities in between embodiments. Light Rays are projected from there to the Earth for specific purposes; such as dissolving epidemics and accumulating destructive forces and also Light Rays are projected into the consciousness of mankind.

The Etheric City over the Sahara Desert is known as the Golden City. Shamballa is over the Gobi Desert. There is an Etheric City over Tucson, Arizona and the Arizona Desert. There is one over Brazil. There is an Etheric City over Glastonbury, England.

Ascended Masters and Beings work from these Etheric Cities and give assistance to mankind in various ways. They may project ideas of some projects which are worthy enough to promote, into the minds of some students who are in physical embodiment. Many Ascended Masters establish and maintain a Focus of Their own in an Etheric City. For example, in the Etheric City over Tucson Arizona, there are Focuses of John the Beloved, the Goddess of Purity, Lord Krishna, and the Seven Holy Kumaras. This gives Them a sort of step-down or in-between action and connection from the high Vibratory Action of Their Ascended Masters' Realm. Around the Etheric Cities is a Force, a Belt or Sphere which nothing of a slower vibration can penetrate.

The "New Jerusalem" is an archetype of Golden Age Etheric Cities of Light that exist even now on the Etheric Plane (in the "Heaven World") and are waiting to be lowered into physical manifestation (on Earth).

In the Book of Revelation, John the Beloved saw the descent of the Holy City as the Immaculate Geometry of that which is to be - and now is in the invisible Realms of Light: "And I John saw the Holy City, New Jerusalem, coming down from God out of Heaven." Thus, in order that this vision and prophecy be fulfilled Jesus taught us to pray with the authority of the Spoken Word, "Thy Kingdom come on Earth as it is in Heaven!"

" . . . From the Etheric City that I AM presently serving in with certain Members of the Great White Brotherhood, We are releasing specialized Rays of Comfort, Peace and Healing for the wounds of this dear planet and her evolutions. It is such a Joyous Experience to be able to see, as the result of your Decrees, the instantaneous Manifestations of Perfection brought about by the Light Rays We send forth to do your and Our bidding, knowing that the Light of God cannot fail!

"While you are yet unascended, your lovely Spirits still encased in the heavier garments of flesh, I know it is more difficult for you than it is for Us to feel the full Glory and Power of the Ascended Ones. Of course, this is because the humanly shadowed thoughts and feelings of fear, frustrated desires, and often bodily pain and other distresses surround the outer self and disturb the peace and poise of your being. These prevent much of your enjoyment of the abundant life that is your Divine Right to experience from coming into manifestation. Besides, these human conditions and conditionings take a heavy toll on your energies by drawing and holding your attention to them.

"If you allow them, they live in your world off of your life, for they really have no world or life or power or volition of their own! Then, too, the beautiful, instantaneous service of the Violet Fire is not so apparent to you as it is to Us when you call It into dynamic action to permanently transmute that which is human to make way for that which is Divine."

"However, if you will 'keep on keeping on', as beloved Saint Germain says, in your sincere endeavor to understand and practice the use of this merciful violet fire, you really can rise very quickly in consciousness to a State of Being where you can see, hear, and associate with the ascended ones long before your actual Ascension takes place. If you really desire this accomplishment enough to hold uninterrupted harmony in your feelings, We can help you to this end. For I had such experiences before My Own Victory was attained.

"O dear hearts, could you but know that each of you is constantly held within an Aura of our Personal God Protection and Loving Care! If you consciously realize and accept this Gift of Our Love by turning your attention to Us every so often during the day, we can cause it to act more readily and powerfully for you.

"There are times when I sincerely wish the Great Cosmic Law would allow Us to remove the veil of unbelief from all mankind by permitting them to have even one glimpse of the magnificent Ascended Masters and angelic realms of Light, which are so real – the exquisite Colors, soul-stirring Melodies, and Joyous Expressions of pure Divine Love that manifest there. Were each lifestream to be able to see such God Splendor even once, it should satisfy that one's consciousness for all eternity that the will of God for all is good and that in the acceptance of and loving cooperation with his will they can be safe at last from every human bondage.

"Believe Me when I say to you from personal experience that the truly indescribable Perfection that We enjoy is worth every effort you have ever made to serve the Light in the appearance world; it is worth every so-called sacrifice of the human you have ever made or ever will make to attain your eternal Victory. . . ."

Beloved Godfre through the Messenger, <u>Mark Prophet</u>, 1958, U.S.A. [2]

References:

1. Luk, A.D.K.   *The Law of Life : Book II* (Pueblo, Colorado: A.D.K. Luk Publications, 1989); pages 413 - 414
2. Godfre, 1958   *Pearls of Wisdom* ®, Volume 1, Number 17 (The Summit Lighthouse ®, 1958) Copyright © 1998 Church Universal and Triumphant ®
3. Krishna, April 4, 1999   *The Temple of The Presence* ®, Parsifal's Victory II, New York City, New York U.S.A. Copyright © 1999 The Temple of The Presence ®

Picture Credits:

Top of page: Adaptation of a still from the movie *What Dreams May Come* © 1998 Interscope Communications, in association with Metafilmics, released by Polygram Filmed Entertainment

An Intentional Community as A City of Light

In preparing to publish The City of Light Sedona, we have spent hundreds of hours researching just about every facet of "cities of light", enlightenment, transformation, earth changes, UFO's, etc. One of the more intriguing web sites that we found is at www.lqcity.com.

Because we desire to share information on resources including concepts that may be of value to anyone who is interested in enlightenment, consciousness and sustainable living, we decided to share some of the introductory information to this planned intentional community. Their stated purpose is to build Cities of Light that will promote love, beauty, compassion, and prosperity.

"According to David Hawkins, MD, PhD, you can only do this by helping people awaken. The best way, he says, is by raising your own Level of Consciousness. What better and more fun way to succeed at that task than by helping to build a town and live in that town with others of like consciousness?"

"We the founders of the Cities of Light believe creativity will be encouraged while synergy, increasing consciousness and power will be produced when people of like mind and of high consciousness do live together in a 'Town of the Future.'"

"We call this town the City of Light or LQ City because residents will have a high Light Quotient. When it is built, the residents will give it a real name, and we will go on to build other Cities of Light throughout the world to raise the consciousness of the world. "

The LQ City of Light's Purpose:

TO BUILD BEAUTIFUL, STIMULATING, ECONOMICALLY VIABLE TOWNS FOR ENLIGHTENED PEOPLE (ABOVE 500 ON HAWKINS' SCALE OF CONSCIOUSNESS) WHICH WILL BE A MODEL FOR THE WORLD.

RATIONALE: THERE IS NEEDLESS ANIMOSITY, MISERY, AND SUFFERING IN THE WORLD. TOO MANY LIVES ARE WASTED. WE ALL CAN BE HEALTHIER, MORE CREATIVE, JOYFUL, AND EVOLVING IN EACH AND EVERY MOMENT. THE CITIES OF LIGHT WILL PROVE THIS TRUE.

OBJECTIVES:

1. TO RAISE CONSCIOUSNESS:

Too few realize what consciousness is, fewer realize its importance. By building a town with residents of high light quotients (above 500) we will publicize the importance of high consciousness.

2. TO CREATE A NEW ECONOMY:

Too few understand or appreciated Buckminster Fuller's quote of 1979: "Technologically we now have four billion billionaires on board Spaceship Earth who are entirely unaware of their good fortune. Unbeknownst to them their legacy is being held in probate by general ignorance, fear, selfishness, and a myriad of paralyzing professional licensing, zoning, building laws, and the like, as bureaucratically maintained by the incumbent power structures."

By building a town that provides a positive environment for entrepreneurs, a win-win situation for all residents, the attitude of caring instead of cut throat competition, and the synergy of creative minds, we will prove Bucky correct.

3. TO IMPROVE MENTAL, PHYSICAL, AND EMOTIONAL HEALTH:

Too few realize that a proper diet, physical exercise, a positive life style, and mental awareness can lead to healthier lives and joy and peace. Too many have blocks in their subconscious minds that prevent any desire to improve.

By building a town where people's subconscious blocks can be cleared, where everyone is encouraged to build a healthy body, and where positive attitudes exist, we will amaze the world.

4. TO POPULARIZE SPIRITUALITY (HIGHER CONSCIOUSNESS):

Too many are ensnared by limiting beliefs or are unaware of their spiritual selves. By building a town with people who live lives of high consciousness, we will awaken the world to the value of spirituality.

5. TO PROMOTE DAVID HAWKINS' BOOK POWER VS FORCE:

Too few realize the importance of this book's main thesis: we all can easily determine the truth and awaken. No longer need the human race be described as "walking dead." By building a town with people above 500 we can help others awaken.

6. TO EXPORT CITIES OF LIGHT:

Too few live in a peaceful yet positive, stimulating environment.
By building a town that works we can export this product to every corner of the earth.

7. TO DEVELOP A NEW APPROACH TO EDUCATION:

Too few of our youth are educated, self disciplined, aware of the truth, or healthy. (According to David Hawkins, 1/3 or earth's population has brain damage because of an inadequate diet or from lack of love and care when they were young.)

By building a town which cares about its young people with a free educational system which truly educates for residents from conception through high school, we will provide a model for the world to emulate.

NOTE: Because The Light Center is based in Sedona where Dr. Hawkins lives and because we also happen to deeply appreciate Dr. Hawkins work, we loved the founders' vision of using his Map of Consciousness and levels of enlightened consciousness to "prequalify" residents. Some of Dr. Hawkins best works are available as Featured Resources from Ultimate Destiny University

Dr. Hawkins' research is based on a well-established science called kinesiology, which has to do with the testing of an all-or-none muscle response stimulus. A positive stimulus generates a strong muscle response, and a negative stimulus results in a demonstrable weakening of the test muscle. Clinical kinesiological muscle testing as a diagnostic technique has been verified widely over the past 25 years.

About the Author

Genii Townsend is an author, trainer, marionette artist, entrepreneur and "trans-audio medium". She owned and operated Geniiland, a 5,000 square foot marionette theater near Hollywood for 18 years.

Genii dropped out of high school and later found herself a divorced mother of a son and daughter trying to figure out how to support them with no office experience and totally no business sense. The answer came in the form of entertaining through the medium of puppets. All she knew was that by being positive and using her Imagination, she could have anything she wanted, which could **be interesting ... and profitable.**

She changed her name from Jean to Genii as it seemed to have magic attached and she needed a lot of that if she was to survive with the children and THE MAGIC HAPPENED! She went on to create a zillion puppets and marionettes and performed professionally from Disneyland to Las Vegas, made commercials funnier, pulled strings in motion pictures and was a co-performer with Carol Burnett on her show with a look-a-like figure of Carol's charwoman Genii had created.

Genii's big dream was to have a birthday party theater where children could have a special place of honor to enjoy. What then began as a tiny storefront theater, expanded four times into a two story 5,000 square foot building where thousands of kids and parents celebrated for 18 years consecutively with many regular fans among famous stars of stage, television and motion pictures.

Genii has been awarded many honors including several by the Puppeteers of America for advancing puppetry, Who's Who in America and NAWBO, the National Association of Women Business Owners. She leads women's self discovery seminars and Playshops such as**:** The Cinderella Connection: Inner Child Healing Doll Classes; The Power Women; and The Thirteen Goddesses of Inner Light. Genii is the author of: *The Little Light Being*; *The Sickness Bug*; *Out of the Gourd-inary ....Plants with an Attitude*; *Conversations About Ultimate Destiny with Who-No, A Spirit Coach*; *Discover the Secrets of How to Grant Your Own Wishes from a Real Genii*, and *The City of Light Sedona*.

Genii is cofounder of The Light Center and Ultimate Destiny University, two non-profit organizations based in Sedona, AZ. One of their present projects is helping create Empowerment Marionettes of world-class authors and trainers to help children harness their creative imagination and realize more of their potential.

Introduction to the Light Center

The LIGHT Center
Love . Imagination . Growth . Healing . True Identity.

Home   Resources   Membership   GLOW   4 Keys   Events   Survey

Genii lives in Sedona, Arizona. She and her business partner Charles Betterton have co-founded two companies (the Imagination Center, Inc. and Imagination Celebration Unlimited LLC) and four non-profit organizations (the Wonderful World of Wishes, Ultimate Destiny University, CENTER SPACE (the Center for Spiritual, Personal And Community Enlightenment and The Light Center.)

Genii delights in creating celebrity marionettes and presenting them to the star so they can pull their own strings. She is now working with Ultimate Destiny University to create "empowerment marionettes" of world- class authors and trainers such as Deepak Chopra, Les Brown, Mark Victor Hansen and celebrities such as Oprah, Whoopi, and Ellen Degeneres to help children of all ages become empowered and learn how to use their creative imagination, Imagine That!

The Light Center, Inc. was established as a non-profit membership organization, partly as a vehicle for accomplishing the task of publishing information on the Sedona City of Light along with other resources for empowerment, enlightenment, healing, consciousness and transformation.

The Sedona City of Light is not for sale. It is Holy and sacred and Genii has been directed to reveal what has been entrusted to her and share this information with others who may be interested.

Genii has granted the copyright for the Sedona City of Light to The Light Center which will help publish and distribute the manuscript. Given the direction to keep the Sedona City of Light Holy and sacred and the reality that it costs money to provide printed materials and audio video content, The Light Center decided to provide electronic copies of The Sedona City of Light on a donation basis.

For the versions of the manuscript that cost money to produce them (such as photo copies of the manuscript, CD ROMS, and printed books as the manuscript is further refined and as funding is available to print the contents as books), The Light Center will list the actual costs to produce the information in various formats. The Light Center will then invite anyone who is interested in receiving a copy to become a member of The Light Center and make a donation to at least cover the actual costs of production and shipping and handling.

Genii has been sharing the wealth of wisdom entrusted to her with others for decades through small group classes, workshops and discussion groups. These resources include: *The 4 Keys to Light; Thirteen Goddesses of Inner Light: GLOW, Gathering Light of Wisdom;* and *Discover the Secrets of How to Grant Your Own Wishes from a Real Genii!*.

Now The Light Center is seeking volunteers to help Genii adapt the training programs she has created to reach and serve many others through the power of the Internet. For example, at least the first 2 of the 4 Keys to Light can be shared electronically.

In addition to transferring the copyright for The Sedona City of Light to The Light Center, Genii has decided to have TLC help her refine, publish, produce and distribute related programs for empowerment and enlightenment.

The Light Center has also made arrangements with several other resource providers for their programs, products and services to be made available to TLC members. For example, the **Ultimate Destiny University for Successful Living** is providing a free copy of its introductory 80 page e-book, Manifesting Your Ultimate Destiny, to all TLC members. Ultimate Destiny is also donating 50% to 100% of the sale of any of its Ultimate Destiny Success System and other present and future programs to TLC members back to The Light Center. More details of the available resources are provided at the end of this document.

The books listed earlier in this manuscript are all available for sale through The Light Center at www.sedonalightcenter.org/featured_resources.htm.

Publications by Genii Townsend

Invitation from Genii and The Light Center

Putting this book together with the profound assistance of my business partner Charles Betterton, Kathie Brodie, and Renee Trenda makes me feel like a female Indiana Jones seeking a treasure unknown. I have witnessed superb visions beyond belief, and to share them with you is a personal blessing. **Thank you!**

I do know, as a student of truth, that in my many playshop sessions, women have been led to become more than they think they are, and they are experiencing a life that is great in all directions, and also that they desire and deserve a higher awareness and healings of various kinds.

In this manuscript I have also included many teachers with their talents who also can lead us. This journey covers a lot of beliefs of mine that I share with you, for whatever you can accept for your own. Is the Sedona City of Light just a mental dream of mine? Perhaps. A wish? Yes, but with that comes a knowing so deep that to see us walking into it is reality that will not be ignored for any reason.

We students walking a path of higher consciousness are aware that miracles do happen, so don't be surprised if one day a City of Light magically appears equipped with vast healing techniques in superb architecture that only God would display for us mortals, to make us believe that peace on earth is indeed probable, and that somewhere in our past we did something right. Yes, God has something wonderful planned for you, me and millions of others who will be shown that Heaven on Earth has appeared and all is well.

It has been my profound pleasure to share and give you a peek into the future that is wonder-filled and where all is healed, for this manuscript contains only a portion of hundreds of pages that have been given to me. I have included questions and answers here, and I will also have questions and answers posted on the blog site. What I have been speaking of is nearer than you know ... or maybe you do? Imagine that! So light it be!

If you resonate at all with the vision presented in The City of Light Sedona, we invite you to help us further refine and share it with the world. If you have created a product or program related to fostering love, light, leadership, awakening, empowerment, enlightenment, healing, etc., we invite you to submit them for possible inclusion as a featured resource from The Light Center. If you know of other resources or references to "cities of light" and or if you have personal stories of interest to share, please join The Light Center and participate in our blog at http://sedonacityoflight.wordpress.com.

Copies of The City of Light Sedona are available for $24.95 from The Light Center at http://www.cityoflightsedona.com and from Ultimate Destiny University at http://www.ultimatedestinyuniversity.org.

Training Programs with Genii

The Four Keys to LIGHT Initiation

Bringing much advancement to the student's path, **The 4 Keys to Light** are an extraordinary and greatly accelerated initiation into higher consciousness. This program assists you in developing the ability to consciously connect and remain connected to your Supreme Light and the higher Light Intelligences that are assisting and guiding your lifestream. You will receive and remember these ancient and most holy teachings that will catapult you into mastery, self empowered knowing, sacred trust and responsibility.

In the first key, you will anchor **The Word**, the most powerful word of Creation to support your mission in the planetary shift and the mastering of dualistic energies. **Atonement** is the harmonic simplicity of tone to align all of your energetic bodies to the rhythms of the Universe. Your guiding forces of Light will make themselves known as you learn to connect to, transmit and use **Divine Intelligence** in your life's mission.

The 4th key is considered the most celebrated moment of your embodiment. The **Light Linkage** will greatly accelerate your advancement, as an open channel of Love, into Oneness as any remaining separations are abolished through the Power of Light.

The most important consideration to anchor these high frequencies of Light unification is to remain in a state of absolute surrender to Divine Will and to use these teachings in your daily devotion. We all must exercise the newly expanded awareness while remembering that our mission is to embody self mastery on every level. With the assistance of **The 4 Keys to Light** program, we deepen our commitment and anchor our mission as Ambassadors of Light.

Genii

The 4 Keys to Light is facilitated by Genii Townsend of Sedona, also known as "the Genii" and Kathie Brodie in Seattle, WA. Genii may be contacted at (928) 284-5566 or by email at thegeniiconnection@msn.com. Kathie may be contacted at miss.brodie@comcast.net. **Tuition for The 4 Keys to Light is on a Love Offering donation basis.**

Kathie

The 4 Keys to Light

The old often repeated saying "When the student is ready, the teacher appears" and so it is with this ancient teaching given in 4 Sacred Keys for modern days usage. The power of the Genie is well known in fables and this Genii is no exception as she brings forth long kept secrets of universal wisdom to elevate and empower those who seek such an advanced leverage.

Since the 4 Keys to Light contain much power and light enhanced information and has, until this time been given to only those who requested an unknown advanced education due to possible misuse of it did they find that teacher with the Genie power readied to be transferred to a student who would take care of it and its use. Thus what could be said is it is one of God's best kept secrets.

From the God self of the Genii and the Kathie Brodie as trans-audio mediums, comes the treasures they have held sacred. The students are enlightened while receiving Light elevations during the sessions while learning of the 4 Keys material.

That includes each student learning of the personal Soul Guides that brought them to this teaching. This is a program not to be missed with all it contains as planetary changes take place.

4 Keys to Light Testimonials:

"I highly recommend Genii Townsend's class on The 4 Keys to Light! She ties together the best advice I have ever seen about getting to know some aspects of your being that you might not have explored before. I have had a running dialogue with God all my life. I have gotten some absolutely wonderful answers to questions, gotten guidance I have asked for, and have enjoyed heavenly energies.

I always thought these answers were coming from my "Higher Self." After The 4 Keys, I came to recognize that indeed much of my contact was with my Higher Self, but a great deal was also coming from my dedicated Spirit Guides that have been with me all of my life. I can now see the difference, and I am in awe of the way that God has created this system within us.

In the class, I also learned to actually USE my 8th chakra. I always knew it was there, but didn't know what to do with it. And ... I learned to use a specific sacred name of God to lovingly clear all negative energies. This really works in a flash, and it is no problem to stay in the Light all of the time with this. I know the 4 Keys Class will be of great benefit to anyone who applies what they learn. It is as fascinating as it is helpful." -- Renee Trenda, Stelle, IL

> **"Are you ready to take the next step in your spiritual journey?** Buckle your seatbelt and get ready for an extraordinary journey into higher consciousness through the "4 Keys to Light" as taught by Genii Townsend of Sedona, Arizona. I was initiated into the 4 Keys by Genii eight years ago at a time when only a select few received these teachings. It's been a nonstop ride of being connected to Universal guidance that one cannot even imagine. At this time, Genii has been guided to impart these teachings to those who are ready and willing to make that next step. I'm certainly glad I did." -- Richard LaDuke

> "Genii took me through the 4 Keys in 2000 and it certainly changed my life. There was a subtle shift at first, then as I traveled farther and farther away from the ceremony I began to notice major shifts that I was able to attribute back to that time. My path became clear, I trusted myself and my guidance more the Universe stepped in to reward me for being open. Life always has its ups and downs but after the 4 Keys I could understand the reasons behind some of the lessons I was getting. That doesn't mean I always liked them, but at least I could accept them. Before the 4 Keys I feel like I was just wandering around but after the Keys there was clarity for me. I can definitely say that having Genii take me through the 4 Keys was a turning point in my life. I wish I had met her years ago!" -- Kathie Brodie, Consulting Hypnotist www.TheBaggageHandler.com

If you are interested in the 4 Keys to Light training in Sedona, AZ, Seattle, WA, Stelle, IL or San Diego, CA, please contact Genii at 928-284-5566. For more details please visit www.sedonalightcenter/org.

The Light Center is presently working on transforming the contents of the 4 Keys to Light training to be able to also offer it online. Two of our affiliated non-profit organizations, Ultimate Destiny University and CENTER SPACE™, are helping us publish and distribute The City of Light Sedona. They are also helping The Light Center develop new ways to share The 4 Keys to Light.

The next few pages provide a brief introduction to the Ultimate Destiny University for Successful Living and CENTER SPACE (the Center for Spiritual, Personal And Community Enlightenment.

Introduction to Ultimate Destinyland™ and Ultimate Destiny University

The shared vision and mission of Ultimate Destiny Network and Ultimate Destiny University are to help "Expand the Circle of Success" for 100% of humankind and to foster personal, organizational, community and planetary empowerment, enlightenment, consciousness and sustainability.

> "Inherently, each one of us has the substance within to achieve whatever our goals and dreams define. What is missing from each of us is the training, education, knowledge and insight to utilize what we already have." - Mark Twain

The world has changed greatly since Mark Twain's time, but individuals still dream and are searching for the training, education, knowledge and insight they need in record numbers. The personal and professional development field has grown to a $210 billion industry and "wellness" is an industry poised to become the next trillion dollar industry according to experts. (www.ultimatesuccesspuzzle.com)

Ultimate Destiny Network is a "cause-oriented" international marketing and distribution company that helps individuals, organizations, and communities accomplish their goals and realize their dreams. The Company has created an innovative business model and Strategic Marketing Matrix System™ that capitalizes on the latest approaches to on-line education, communication and marketing; synergistic alliances with other industry providers; as well as collaborations with key government and national nonprofit organizations.

Ultimate Destiny University (UDU) is a non-profit membership organization that produces, publishes, markets and distributes materials designed to empower people, deepen spirituality, and awaken them to conscious, sustainable living. In actuality, UDU is a collection of intellectual properties consisting of domain names, websites, blogs, e-books, print books, e-courses, e-zines, membership programs, webinars, teleseminars, audio CDs, and video DVDs all created to help people **A.R.K.** -- **A**waken to Spirit; **R**ealize more of their potential; and **K**now how to cocreate their ultimate destiny (whatever that means to each individual).

Because we believe The City of Light Sedona will play such a major role in helping us fulfill our personal and global "ultimate destinies" we are deeply grateful for the opportunity to help Genii Townsend and The Light Center

For more information on any facet of Ultimate Destinyland, please contact Charles Betterton at 760-212-9931 or ceo@ultimatedestinyuniversity.com.
www.ultimatedestinyland.com   www.ultimatedestinyuniversity.org

Featured Resources from Ultimate Destinyland™

Which Pieces of Solving Your Ultimate Destiny Success Puzzle Are Most Important To You?

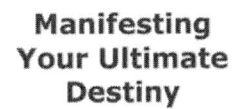

Manifesting Your Ultimate Destiny 	**Solving Your Ultimate Destiny Success Puzzle** 	**Enjoying Financial Freedom and Prosperity** 	**Achieving Ultimate Business and Career Success** 
Fulfilling Your Life Purpose and Mission 	**Realizing Your Ultimate Potential** 	**Harnessing Your Creative Mind Power** 	**Enjoying Loving Relationships** 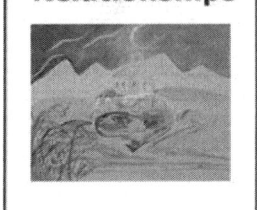
Enjoying Peace and Balance 	**Raising Your Level of Consciousness** 	**Enjoying Ultimate Health and Fitness** 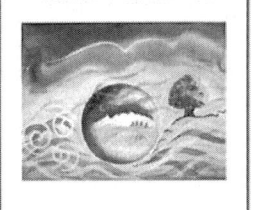	**Attaining Spiritual Enlightenment** 
Making A Difference Leaving A Legacy 	**Fostering Personal and Planetary Sustainability** 	**Solving Our Personal, Community and Global Success Puzzles** 	**Discover the Secrets of How to Cocreate Your Ultimate Destiny!** 

210

Introduction to CENTER SPACE™ Resources

CENTER SPACE (the Center for Spiritual, Personal And Community Enlightenment) is a nonprofit membership organization established to help foster spiritual, personal and community empowerment and enlightenment. **CENTER SPACE** provides programs, products and services that help people, organizations and communities **A.R.K. -- A**waken to their true spiritual identity, **R**ealize more of their potential and **K**now how to fulfill their ultimate destiny (whatever that means to each individual).

CENTER SPACE, Inc. was incorporated for the following specific purposes:

✓ To provide educational programs and materials that foster spiritual, personal, organizational and community development, empowerment and enlightenment

✓ To foster greater communication, cooperation and understanding among people of different races, cultures, religions and socio-economic levels

✓ To facilitate cooperative and creative problem solving efforts between individuals, businesses, religious organizations, non-profit organizations and government

✓ To develop models for establishing **CENTER SPACE** facilities in other areas

CENTER SPACE seeks to help the Ultimate Destiny University for Successful Living manifest Bucky Fuller's vision of "betterment for 100% of humanity." We plan to do that by helping people, organizations and communities empower themselves, realize more of their potential and expand their capacity to help address the increasing social, environmental and economic challenges we face on SpaceShip Earth.

Our ultimate goal is to help Expand the Circle of Success be establishing an international network of CAN DO! Centers for Successful Living that will provide Successful Living Skills for the 21st Century that will help Solve Personal, Community, National and Global Success Puzzles. The shared vision of Expanding the Circle of Success™ is to facilitate the distribution and donation of 100 million dollars worth of resources for personal, organizational and community empowerment, enlightenment and transformation through an international infrastructure of thousands of locally initiated Empowerment Resource Centers™ by 2012.

If you resonate with the vision of helping people Awaken to Spirit, Realize More of Their Potential and Know How to Manifest Their Ultimate Destiny, please contact CENTER SPACE, PO Box 20072, Sedona, AZ 86341. Our email address is centerspaceinc@gmail.com. * www.centerspace.com

Examples of Programs Available from CENTER SPACE:

Motivision — 21 Steps to Manifest Your Ultimate Vision	**Developing Spiritually Centered New Year's Resolutions**	**Partnership with God**	**T.U.L.I.P.S.** — The Ultimate Life Inpowerment Planning System — A Comprehensive Spiritually Oriented Program for Achieving Personal and Professional Goals
Peace! Be Still and Know God	**Rise and Shine!** With Seven Ascension Attitudes	**Seven Ascension Attitudes**	**Your Interview with God, the Ultimate Entrance Exam**
The Five Steps of Spiritual Mind Treatment — Dr. Ernest Holmes — There is a Power for Good in the Universe Greater Than You Are and You Can Use It.	**CROWNED WITH THE ULTIMATE SUCCESS OF THE LORD!** — Seven Ascension Attitudes – That Help You A.R.K. Awaken to Your Spiritual Identity, Realize More of Your Potential and Know How to Cocreate Your Ultimate Destiny!	**Godhood, Who Me? Oh My God!**	**Spiritual Prosperity Treasure Chest**
Empowerment 101 — Resources to Help You Discover How to Realize More of Your Potential and Enjoy A Happier, Richer and More Fulfilling Life!	**Enlightenment 101** — Where Are You on the Enlightenment Ladder?	**S.P.A.R.K. of Destiny** — Our Spiritual Purpose is to Awaken to Our Spiritual Identity of Divinity, Realize More of Our Potential for Godhood, Know How to Cocreate Our Ultimate Destiny! — Charles Betterton	**Discovering and Manifesting Our Dreams with Co-Creative Visioning**

Made in the USA
Charleston, SC
03 February 2012